CUSTOM MADE

A CATALOGUE OF PERSONALIZED AND HANDCRAFTED ITEMS

Sheila Buff

MACMILLAN PUBLISHING COMPANY
New York

COLLIER MACMILLAN PUBLISHERS
London

A RUNNING HEADS BOOK

Copyright © 1990 by Running Heads Incorporated

Macmillan Publishing Company
866 Third Avenue
New York, NY 10022
Collier Macmillan Canada, Inc.

Library of Congress Cataloging-in-Publication Data
Buff, Sheila.
    Custom made / Sheila Buff, Running Heads, Inc.
        p.   cm.
    ISBN 0-02-605960-6
    1. Handicraft industries—United States.   2. Handicraft—United
States.   3. Customer service—United States.   I. Running Heads,
Inc.   II. Title.
HD2346.U5B79   1990
745.5′068—dc20   90-31014
                                                            CIP

Macmillan books are available at special discounts for bulk purchases for sales promotions, premiums, fund-raising, or educational use. For details, contact:

> Special Sales Director
> Macmillan Publishing Company
> 866 Third Avenue
> New York, NY 10022

CUSTOM MADE
was conceived and produced by Running Heads Incorporated
55 West 21 Street
New York, NY 10010

Editor: Charles de Kay
Designer: Sue Rose
Managing Editor: Lindsey Crittenden
Production Manager: Linda Winters
Photo Researcher: Ellie Watson

10 9 8 7 6 5 4 3 2 1

Typeset by Trufont Typographers Inc.
Color Separations by Hong Kong Scanner Craft Company
Printed in Singapore through Palace Press, New York.

This one's for Mom and Dad.

ACKNOWLEDGMENTS

Many, many people generously shared their time and expertise with me as I sought out custom products. I am deeply grateful to everyone who responded to my letters and calls and agreed to participate in this book. In addition, I must thank those who pointed me in the right direction: Sandy Blye, American Fur Industry; Casey Bush, Millinery Information Bureau; John Cergol, National Spa & Pool Institute; Jean Dalury, Timberpeg; William Fioravanti; Diane Fisher, Diane Designs; Jean Harper, International Pastry Arts Center; Smitty Kogan and Jean-Louis Carbonnier, Champagne News and Information Bureau; Cele Lalli, *Modern Bride* magazine; John Lamm for advice on cars; Irma Lipkin, Custom Tailors & Designers Association of America; Nick Lyons, Lyons & Burford, for advice on fly rods; Suzanne Maggin, bridal consultant; Anthony Maurizio; Tony Meisel for advice on boats; Linda Miller, American Federation of Astrologers; Frank Mowery, Guild of Book Workers; Ed Pavelka, *Bicycling* magazine; Keith Pilgrim for advice on travel; Catha Rambusch, Rambusch Studios; Dr. Jeffrey Starr, Bijan; Andy Tarshis, Tiecrafters; and all the other people who patiently answered my questions, shared their knowledge, and passed me on to an ever-widening network of experts and artisans.

Josephine Bacon and Kate Russell-Cobb, friends and colleagues in England, very kindly assisted my research there.

Charlie de Kay of Running Heads provided valuable editorial suggestions and support; Ellie Watson provided help in the picture research. As always, all the staff at Running Heads were unfailingly cheerful and helpful. Miriam Sarzin did her usual fine job of copyediting the manuscript. Thanks are also due to Elisa Petrini of Macmillan for her faith in this unusual project.

CONTENTS

In the course of researching and writing this book, the question of exactly what is meant by custom made was raised frequently. It has no easy answer. Generally, custom made means exactly that: something crafted by a talented specialist exclusively for the client. This definition covers, more or less broadly, most of the topics—from apparel to umbrellas—included here. For the purposes of the book it has been further expanded to include objects produced slowly with painstaking hand craftsmanship (Rolls-Royce automobiles, for instance) or in limited editions (collector's dolls, for example). Objects that are handcrafted to standard patterns in such a way that each object is unique even though the design is not (handpainted tiles, for one) also fall under the above definition. Because unusual and exclusive services (safari planning, for example) are tailored to the specific individual, they can also be considered custom made.

A related and perhaps more difficult question is where to draw the line between a custom-made craft object and a commissioned work of fine art. Here the definition rests primarily on function: as a rule but not always, the custom-made products in this book are useful as well as beautiful. This means, for example, that quilts and rugs are included but wall hangings are not, although all of those are made by equally talented fiber artists.

The goal of *Custom Made* is to present a sampling of the finest custom products available today. The craftspeople and companies discussed and illustrated here have well-established reputations for talent and integrity; they can handle orders and commissions from anywhere in the country. To reach them, use the Resources section at the back of the book.

This section provides information about nearly four hundred makers of custom products. Generally, the listing will put you into direct contact with the producer. The listing in some cases (wristwatches, for example) gives the address and phone number of the company headquarters; the staff there can usually provide further information and can tell you where you can order or purchase the product in your area. Some products and services (swimming pools and genealogists, for example) are best arranged for through local sources. In those cases, the Resources listing provides information about national organizations that can refer you to competent people in your area.

Finding just the right craftsperson for the item you want is not always easy. A good way to begin is by visiting crafts shows. Local crafts shows are a good way to meet the craftspeople in your area. On a wider basis, many regional crafts shows are sponsored by crafts organizations such as American Craft Enterprises. These shows are usually juried—that is, the participants must submit their work to and be accepted by a jury of experts before they can participate. Because exhibitors at juried crafts shows tend to be more established, and because exhibitors at regional shows will be drawn from a wider geographic area, these shows are good places to find talented custom workers in many different fields. Galleries, advertisements in special-interest magazines, design sourcebooks, and word-of-mouth (the best advertising anyone can have) are also excellent ways to find crafts workers.

Once the search has been narrowed down, talk seriously with the candidates. Explain as completely as you can exactly what you want (pictures of similar

Sonance custom-designs and installs built-in architectural audio systems, opposite page. The speakers and controls are matched to the room's design.

Sculptor Wendy Ross at work on the clay model for her monumental bronze portrait of the late Congressman Phillip Burton; left.

pieces, rough sketches, and an idea of the dimensions are useful) and explain exactly how much you are willing to spend (remember that shipping expenses for large items are usually charged to the customer). Ask to see the artist's portfolio and for any other information he or she can provide: an exhibition list, resume, brochure and so on. Always make sure to ask for references from previous clients, and always follow up on them for information.

Given the extent and ease of modern communications and shipping, most craftspeople will accept commissions from anywhere. Unless the project involves something that needs fitting (a suit, for example) or that can't be shipped (a floor, for example), there is often little real need to meet face to face with the artist—sketches, color swatches and other details can all be sent through the mail and discussed over the telephone. On the other hand, sharing your ideas with a master craftsperson and watching them take shape is one of the most enjoyable aspects of having something custom made, and for that reason alone you may prefer to work with artists you can visit conveniently while the project is underway.

The Resources section includes some individuals and companies that are not discussed in the text or the captions. There are several reasons for this. Some could not provide the necessary materials; others provided information too late to be included in the text. In some areas (furniture, for example) the large number of talented workers meant that there simply wasn't room to discuss everyone. Some fascinating areas,

such as jewelry, stained glass, and pottery, could not be included here. Each of these topics is easily a book in itself. Rather than attempt to select from the many, many fine artists working in these and other areas, it was decided to omit them altogether.

Custom-made products are usually not inexpensive. Surprisingly, however, they are often not much more expensive than the equivalent manufactured products or good antiques. The difference in cost is more than compensated by having something that is beautifully crafted, very durable, and *exactly* what you want. In addition, a custom-made object may well appreciate in value considerably over the years.

No book of this sort can ever hope to be exhaustive, and there are doubtless some glaring omissions. All the topics were extensively researched, using design sourcebooks, trade associations and journals, crafts directories, and a number of other print sources. Experts in various fields were consulted. In addition, many of the people who were contacted very generously shared their knowledge and referred their colleagues. Based on all this, well over a thousand letters requesting information were sent. The responses were many and enthusiastic, but not everyone who responded was included. Some were not really making custom products; others simply weren't good enough. In addition, some people asked *not* to be included, saying that they already had more work than they could handle. In the end, the criteria for inclusion were simple: uniqueness, quality, utility, and beauty.

CHAPTER 1

APPAREL AND ACCESSORIES

Brian Lishak of Wells of Mayfair Ltd. in London displays some examples of bespoke, or custom-made, suits in progress.

The modern business suit worn by today's man has roots over two centuries deep in the English countryside. As the passion for fox-hunting grew among the aristocracy toward the end of the eighteenth century, knee breeches, periwigs, and three-cornered hats gave way to the more practical trousers, coats, and bowler hats. The trend accelerated into a rage when Beau Brummell, arbiter of fashion at the start of the 1800s, decreed that trousers, cravats, and simple coats were what an English gentleman wore. By the 1840s, the styles of modern business attire had evolved, changing in details but not fundamentals ever since.

The advantages of a custom-made suit are many. Surprisingly, a custom suit is not necessarily all that much more expensive than a designer-label ready-to-wear suit purchased at an exclusive menswear store. In the end a custom suit may well be more economical. The classic styling, outstanding fabric, and beautiful construction of a custom suit mean that it can be comfortably and stylishly worn for a long time—anywhere from five to twenty years or more. Most importantly, however, custom-made suits *fit*. No one has a perfect physique, but good tailoring can improve on nature considerably. Most men, for example, have one shoulder slightly lower than the other; proper tailoring can make them look even. Middle-aged paunches, poor posture, bowlegs, and other imperfections can all be discreetly covered by the custom tailor. All the careful measurements taken by the tailor are translated onto a unique paper pattern, which is then used to cut the fabric (always the finest wool worsteds) to the exact size. The pattern, with its fitting modifications, is kept on file so that later suits can be made from it. It is in the cutting that the true art of the fine tailor can be seen. Adjust-ments as minor as a quarter of an inch can make all the difference between good fit and perfect fit.

Much, if not all, of the complicated sewing of a custom suit is done by hand. It can take four hours to do the interior padding stitches of a jacket, which give it its shape and resilience—a process done by machine in under four minutes on rack suits. In the end, more than fifty hours of skilled labor will go into sewing the suit, ending with such important finishing details as a perfectly matched silk lining and four cuff buttons with buttonholes that open on each sleeve. (The origin of cuff buttons is obscure, and why they should open has never been explained. Supposedly Napoleon ordered buttons sewn onto uniforms to keep his soldiers from wiping their noses on their sleeves.)

If cared for properly, a custom

Savile Row is host to some of the finest tailors, including Norton & Sons Ltd., left. This firm has been at this address for over 160 years. Tailor Giacomo Trabalza, below, discusses fabrics with a client.

suit will give many years of service. The secret is regular brushing to remove the dirt, dust, and grit that accumulates in the fabric. The suit should not be worn for more than a day at a time, and should be "rested" for several days (a week if possible) between wearings. Hang it on a curved, shaped hanger; this will reduce the need for pressing. Always empty the pockets before hanging the suit. Most custom tailors offer expert maintenance and cleaning as part of their service. If possible, return the suit to its maker for cleaning; poor dry-cleaning can ruin a suit.

THE CUSTOM TAILORS

London's Savile Row was in full swing by the 1840s as *the* place for the best in bespoke, or custom, tailoring. The finest wools, classic styling, careful fitting, and the best craftsmanship made suits from Savile Row tailors the standard for the world. That standard is upheld today by the many venerable tailoring firms still on Savile Row. Happily for the well-

13

dressed American man, however, many of these companies now send representatives to major American cities several times a year. Indeed, as much as 70 percent of all Savile Row business now comes from Americans. Styles and fabrics are selected and measurements taken on one visit, fittings are done on the next, and delivery follows in due course. Two well-known English firms doing extensive business in America are Wells of Mayfair and Norton & Sons Ltd. Wells of Mayfair has been at the same address since 1829. The firm annually produces suits for customers in more than twenty countries. Also available are bespoke shirts, dress wear, overcoats, hunt clothes, and leisure and sporting wear. Ladies' tailored suits and blouses are another specialty. America is the primary market for Norton & Sons Ltd., a firm that dates back to 1821. Representatives travel to the United States six times a year, visiting clients in eighteen cities.

American custom tailors give Savile Row some stiff competition, offering the same fine fabrics,

One aspect of tailoring is the pattern, where adjustments that ensure a perfect fit are made. The patterns behind Giacomo Trabalza, above, record the measurements of every client.

styles, and workmanship at comparable prices. Most of the true custom tailors belong to the Custom Tailors and Designers As-

sociation of America (the oldest trade organization in the United States). Among them are William Fioravanti and Anthony Maurizio of New York, Joseph Montopoli and Joseph Morrone of Chicago, Ralph DeConto of Boston, and Giacomo Trabalza of Los Angeles. These tailors will also make business suits for women.

Many well-regarded suit manufacturers such as Oxxford, Norman Hilton, and Hickey-Freeman offer the next best thing to custom-made clothing—made-to-measure suits. In this case personal measurements are taken, but the suit is based on a standard model; the client's choice of fabrics is limited. Some fine retailers such as Brooks Brothers and Saint Laurie also offer made-to-measure suits for both men and women.

The two by-appointment-only Bijan boutiques, one on Rodeo Drive in Beverly Hills and the other on Fifth Avenue in New York City, offer what may be the world's most exclusive menswear. Amid incredibly elegant surroundings, Bijan's clients (who include a large number of extremely well-known personages) select their apparel in a luxurious, very private atmosphere. Bijan himself creates every theme and detail in his work and oversees its careful production from the finest materials. He is virtually the only menswear de-

signer in the world who can create quite literally everything his clients wear, from designing the fabric to blending his own cologne.

SHIRTS

A custom-made suit deserves to be complemented by a shirt that fits properly. Custom-made shirts are often available through the same tailors and retailers who provide the suits. The Custom Shop has numerous branches across the country; this chain specializes in shirts for men and women, and also offers custom suits.

Complex sewing, padding, pressing, and other procedures are part of the fifty or more hours of skilled handcraftsmanship needed to create a fine custom suit, above.

15

SHOES

In addition to custom services, the Allen-Edmonds Company offers handcrafted shoes in 186 different sizes, right. The craftsmen at R.E. Tricker Ltd. of London have produced classically styled shoes, below, and boots since 1829.

Classic style and quality make handcrafted shoes the choice of fashion-conscious men; comfort and durability make them the choice of all men. Handmade shoes are the last bastion of full leather construction, making them very important to people (including children) who are allergic to synthetic materials.

More than two hundred different steps can go into making a fine pair of men's shoes by hand, but the basic marks of quality are easy to spot. Finely grained calfskin leather is the first characteristic. Fine calfskin is very durable, and it also "breathes" well, an important comfort factor. Full welting is the next indication of quality. A welt is the leather piece that holds the insole, outsole, and shoe upper together. The welt is the foundation of the shoe; it allows for years of wear and lets the foot flex in the most natural way. It's visible on the shoe as the quarter-inch-thick leather layer at the very top of the sole. In the best shoes, the welting extends completely around the shoe. The other parts of the shoe should be made entirely of leather: base, heel, sole, insole, and lining. A full-length layer of cork between the insole and the outsole will give extra comfort and warmth.

The best-made shoe in the world is worthless unless it fits properly. Ideally, the ball joint of the foot (the widest part of the foot) will be positioned at the widest part of the shoe; thus both will flex at the same point. There should also be at least a half-inch of clearance for the toes at the front of the shoe. In addition, everyone's feet have their own minor peculiarities—most people have one foot slightly larger than the other, for example. The custom shoemaker takes careful measurements, noting all the idiosyncrasies of the feet; he may also ask to see a pair of the client's most comfortable and well-worn shoes. The measurements are transferred to the last (the wooden form on which the shoe is crafted), which is hand-carved and kept for future orders in that particular style; for shoes of a different style, a new fitting is needed and a new last must be made. Other artisans cut the leather, put together the upper, create the sole and heel and finish the shoe.

Handcrafted slippers from Tricker's, right, are made of velvet emblazoned with gold wire.

CARING FOR SHOES

After several wearings (or whenever they become dull and dirty), clean your shoes with a cleaner/conditioner. Apply the product and then wipe with a damp cloth. Let the shoes dry at room temperature, then polish them using a product containing carnauba wax. Buff the shoes with a smooth cloth to bring the finish to a fine luster. This keeps the shoes in good shape. Wearing the same shoes constantly will eventually damage the leather through accumulated dampness. Rotate your shoes, giving them a breather of a day or two between wearings. To help maintain the shape of the shoes, always use shoe trees.

THE SHOEMAKERS

Handmade English shoes have long had a fine reputation. American clients are so important to companies such as John Lobb, Foster & Son, and Tricker's that they send representatives to the United States several times a year. Because the last must be hand-carved for perfect fit, the wait for a pair of these classically styled shoes can be months, but the end result is certainly worth it (the wait for additional shoes on the same last is somewhat shorter). Bootmaker by appointment to both Her Majesty Queen Elizabeth II and His Royal Highness the Prince of Wales, John Lobb Ltd. is the epitome of British shoemakers. In addition to shoes of all sorts (including ladies' golf shoes), this famous firm makes velvet slippers, jodhpur boots, and riding boots—all at breathtaking prices. Five generations of bootmakers have been part of Tricker's of London, starting in 1829—the year of the first varsity boat race between Ox-

ford and Cambridge, and the year Robert Peel founded the London Metropolitan Police. Custom-made shoes from Tricker's are available in a wide range of styles, including formal and business shoes, riding boots for men and women, sandals, and a number of fully waterproof leisure styles for country wear. Foster & Son is noted for traditional styles, particularly hunting boots and classic oxfords and brogues. The firm also crafts exquisite leather luggage, cases, and other leather accessories.

Some American firms also produce stylish custom-made shoes. Among them are The Cordwainer Shop, which also makes women's shoes, the Alden Shoe Company, and T.O. Dey. Allen-Edmonds Shoe Corporation is better known for excellent manufactured shoes, but handles special custom orders.

COWBOY BOOTS

Craftsmen at Tony Lama have made boots for several Presidents, starting with Harry Truman. In 1981, the company made four pairs featuring the Presidential seal, left, for Ronald Reagan. Made-to-measure riding boots, opposite page, by E. Vogel are worn by members of equestrian teams and leading riders worldwide.

The cowboys who drove cattle along the Chisholm Trail from Texas to Kansas in the 1860s needed a new sort of boot, one that could withstand the rigors of life in the saddle. Enterprising cobblers in west Texas soon obliged them, taking the cowboys'

About thirteen square feet of the finest leather go into a pair of Nocona boots; right. The steel shank is padded with rubber and held in place with wooden pegs.

measurements as they passed through town heading north and delivering the boots to the cowboys on the return trip. The boots they made had pointy toes that were easy to slip into the stirrups, and high heels and steel-shanked arches to help keep them in.

The long tradition of custom bootmaking for demanding customers continues today. One of the most famous of all the bootmakers is Charlie Dunn. A third-generation Irish bootmaker, Dunn retired in 1986 on his eighty-eighth birthday. His shop, Texas Traditions, carries on his fine craftsmanship under the guidance of his former apprentice Lee Miller. Boots from Texas Traditions are in great demand, and a wait of six months is normal.

The Tony Lama Company dates back to 1911, when Tony Lama, Sr., completed his cavalry enlistment at Fort Bliss, Texas. Trained as a cobbler in Syracuse, New York, he decided to stay in Texas and enjoy the warm climate. He set up shop as a bootmaker and quickly developed a reputation for quality. The business grew, and Tony's sons joined in. Growth after World War II was rapid, and

soon many celebrities were wearing Tony Lama boots. In addition to entertainment personalities, Tony Lama boots have been worn by top hands such as Lyndon Johnson, Harry Truman, Hubert Humphrey, Ronald Reagan, and Pope John Paul II.

John Wayne got his boots from Lucchese; actor Robert Duvall got his boots for the television production of *Lonesome Dove* from Wheeler Boot Company. Func-

tional boots are still a major concern for all the bootmakers, but decorative boots that make a personal statement are at the heart of the custom business. Exotic leathers such as alligator, java lizard, ostrich, buffalo, and even python are often used in the fanciest cowboy boots.

Caring for all these exotic skins isn't difficult. For the most part, they should be treated just as fine shoes are, with a good cream po-

lish and leather conditioner. Dust and dirt will collect between the scales of reptile skins. This can be removed with a foaming cleaner and conditioner designed to lift the deposits out.

When wearing a pair of boots, remember that cowboys ride horses and Cadillacs. If you'll have to walk more than the length of the parking lot, do your feet a favor and leave your boots at home in the closet.

HANDCRAFTED APPAREL

Tim Harding dyes, layers, quilts, slashes, and frays his all-cotton fabrics to create beautiful combinations of color, texture, and pattern. A coat with shawl collar and fold-back cuffs is shown at left.

If you're planning for a special occasion that requires formal wear, such as the Academy Awards or the Inaugural Ball, you might wish to have an evening gown made for you by a famed couturier such as Scaasi, Nolan Miller, or Bob Mackie. This stratospheric approach to clothing is far beyond the needs of the average woman. You can still have custom-made clothing, which is practical, durable, and beautiful, without spending a fortune.

The explosive new interest in American crafts is exemplified by the people working in fiber arts. Using a fascinating variety of techniques and materials, these artists create clothing that is handmade, sometimes in the most literal sense of the word: Some artists spin and dye their own yarn, weave it into cloth, and then stitch the clothing. Those who work with silk use this fabric's affinity for brilliant dyes to create richly colored designs or actual paintings. Others create knitted clothing, or use silk-screening on silk or cotton. No matter what the medium, all create fashionable apparel that is unique, individually designed, and made to order, often entirely by hand. Apparel made from these exquisite fabrics tends to be fashionably simple. The designers often prefer to work with the natural drape of the fabric, and so tend toward designs that are soft

Fiber artist Suzi Kurtz works with shibori, a Japanese dying technique in which silk is tied, folded, twisted, stitched, or clamped to resist the dyes, left.

and flowing. There is little use of such tailoring techniques used in men's and women's suits as padding, interfacing, stiffening, and the like. These techniques work well with smooth, thin wool worsteds and synthetic fibers, giving them a tailored look. However, these techniques are often not appropriate for fine silks or for heavier, textured fabrics.

Aside from the sheer beauty of the fabrics, there are some good reasons for wearing custom-crafted apparel. The fabrics and styles offered by some artists are on the cutting edge of contemporary fashion; alternatively, other artists are willing to create more traditional clothing for their clients. Custom designs mean that women who usually have trouble finding clothes that fit properly can enjoy elegant clothing. And because these artists work with natural fabrics, their clothing is durable, comfortable, and ecologically sound.

Custom-made business suits for women can be made by the same tailors who create them for men (see the section on custom tailors). Fine stores specializing in women's business attire usually offer custom fitting and alterations. By the same token, fine department and specialty stores often provide custom fitting for evening gowns.

This bias-cut gown and cocoon evening coat, left, were designed and constructed by Suzi Kurtz. The ensemble features hand-overcast seams, a china silk lining and an organza yoke, beaded with pearls.

Using luxury yarns and such natural fibers as mohair, silk, and linen, designer Robin Bergman creates sumptuous hand-loomed and knitted clothing, left.

23

SCARVES

Contemporary designs in unique and limited editions are hand-painted on silk charmeuse, left, by fabric artist Sharon Adee.

With dyes from Paris and the finest silks from around the world, Linda and David Hartge of Kaleidosilk make one-of-a-kind painted scarves and other silk clothing, below.

Scarves make great fashion accents. To get exactly the *right* scarf, you could mount a long and frustrating search through retail stores—or you could have one custom made. Alternatively, you could view these scarves as wearable art and search for outfits to accent them.

Silk is the fabric of choice among many fabric artists, and for good reason. Soft, lustrous, and durable, silk can be beautifully dyed in brilliant colors. Artists such as Marliss Jensen or Linda and David Hartge of Kaleidosilk paint with dyes, using a variety of methods. Other artists, such as Randall Darwall, Juanita Girardin, and Eleanor Voutselas of Panoply weave the dyed silken threads into eye-catching patterns. Combinations of silk with wool and rayon are common, and some artists also work in wool, cotton, and other fabrics. In all cases, because the scarves are hand-painted or hand-woven, even the same design made twice will be different each time. These are truly one-of-a-kind pieces.

Weaver and designer Nancy Lubin creates hand-loomed throws and shawls from luxury fibers such as silk, alpaca, and merino, left.

Randall Darwall's signature fabrics result from combining unusual yarns of silk and other fine fibers, evocative colors, and a variety of complex weave structures, above.

French-born milliner Carine Fraley of Chapeaux Carine produces custom-made hats from her atelier, left. Vanessa Alssid's hat designs, opposite page, embody the look for the 1940s and 1950s for the fashion-aware woman of the 1990s.

There was a time when no well-dressed lady or gentleman went out without a hat, regardless of the weather. Every neighborhood had a millinery shop that made women's hats to order, drawing on a full stock of fabrics, trimmings, and adornments. Hats as an essential part of attire went into eclipse in the 1960s, but today hats for women are making a strong comeback. So are the custom hat makers—a new generation of imaginative, trendy designers is at work.

Men's hats have not fared as well. Custom hats for men are virtually extinct, but Michael Harris of Paul's Hat Works—the last custom hat shop in San Francisco—carries on. Harris makes Panama hats the old-fashioned way—he weaves them by hand and trims them with ribbons dating from before World War II. Despite its name, the Panama hat actually originated in Ecuador; American engineers working on the Panama Canal in 1914 brought the hats back with them and the association with Panama stuck. Today Michael Harris sells his Panamas by mail order all over the world.

Unconventional and eye-catching hats by Sarah Gavaghan feature unusual trims and shapes, above.

So much complex hand work by skilled craftspeople goes into any fur coat that, in effect, they are all custom made—no two are ever exactly alike. Indeed, the fur industry is one of the last to rely almost entirely on hand skills, and fur workers are the highest paid in the entire garment business.

The purchaser of a fur coat today has a choice of over fifty different kinds of fur, coming from more than twenty countries. The majority of furs come from farms or ranches where animals are raised for their fur, just as other animals are raised for their meat. Most mink, rabbit, and fox is ranched, and all nutria, chinchilla, Persian lamb, and broadtail is.

When selecting a fur garment, the most important step is to find a company in which you have complete confidence. In addition to using the suggestions outlined in the Introduction to research furriers, check for the following signs of quality, which a reputable retailer should routinely demonstrate. Does the store offer a complete money-back guarantee if you are not completely satisfied? Does the staff seem respectful of the fact that your purchase is a major investment? Did they answer all your questions openly and patiently? Were you fitted with care? Did the staff give you the opportunity to take your time to decide about making a purchase? (A reputable retailer will never pressure you into a decision.) Do they offer a fur storage service? Would you feel comfortable bringing the fur back to the store for repairs or alterations?

Fur terminology is complicated and occasionally arcane. For the consumer, the confusion is considerably lessened by the Federal label law, which requires every fur product to have a label listing the following information:

28

This Scanblack Saga Mink coat, opposite page, left, was designed by G. Michael Hennessy Furs. Mink wears well and is a good choice for fur coats that will be worn often. The designer for this Golden Island Saga Fox coat, opposite page, right, was Michael Forrest. There are over forty natural shades of fox.

This magnificent Black Diamond® mink coat, left, is available through Evans, the world's largest retail furrier.

• *Name of the fur.* The fur's true name in English must be given. For example, muskrat cannot be called "mink-dyed" muskrat, only dyed muskrat.

• *Country of origin.* If a fur is imported, the country of origin must be given. This means that Canadian sable cannot be passed off as the finer Russian sable.

• *Processing.* This information states whether the fur has been sheared, dyed, or otherwise processed—that is to say, whether the natural texture and color have been at all altered. It should be noted, however, that unprocessed fur is not necessarily any "better" than processed fur.

You should also look for the Fur Label Authority tag on any fur garment. This means the garment was made by a manufacturer who supports the industry code of fair labor standards, and also guarantees that the product was not made from the fur of an endangered species.

Choosing the right type of fur depends on the use it will get. Furs such as mink, raccoon, beaver, and Alaska fur seal are long-wearing, and thus are well suited for all-around garments that will be used often. Other furs, such as broadtail, are more fragile, and are best used only on special occasions. In any case, the better the quality, the better the fur will wear. The best furs have a lustrous, uniform color in the pelts, dense fur, a silky texture, and soft, pliable leather.

CARING FOR FURS

To keep a fur looking its best through years of wear, it must be professionally cleaned at least once a year, even if the garment is not worn often. A fur attracts dust particles even if it is just hanging in the closet. If the fur is not cleaned, the dust will cause the individual hairs to split and break off. Never try to remove spots from fur your-self—this is a job for a professional. If possible, bring the fur back to the store where it was purchased for cleaning.

Fur must be put in professional storage during the warm months. Your furrier has a cold storage vault where temperature, humidity, and air circulation are maintained at the optimal levels.

Damage to a fur—rips, torn seams, loose buttons, and anything else—must be dealt with immediately by a professional. If they are neglected, they will quickly worsen and lead to the expense of a major repair. Check your fur carefully after every wearing, particularly the shoulders, closures, pockets, and the entire back area (this part is especially vulnerable to tears).

Hang your fur coat on a padded hanger, and give it plenty of room in the closet to keep it from being crushed. Never cover it with a plastic bag. If the fur gets wet from rain or snow, hang it on a padded hanger in an airy place away from direct heat such as a radiator. When the fur is dry, just give it a shake and it's ready to wear again. Never use a brush or comb on the fur. Avoid unnecessary friction: don't carry a shoulder bag, and exercise caution getting in and out of cars. Don't pin jewelry or flowers to the fur, and never apply any perfume to it.

29

The most luxurious possible fabrics go into wedding gowns from Carolina Herrera, right: silk satin, jacquard, shantung, crepe, organza, velvet, lace, and tulle.

For many women, the bridal gown she wears is a statement of all that she is and hopes to be. It must be perfect.

Perfection is hard to find, but the makers of couture bridal gowns make the search a little easier. *Long* before the wedding day, start looking through the pages of bridal magazines. You'll see dozens of advertisements for exquisite gowns designed by couturiers such as Carolina Herrera, Bob Mackie and Robert Legere (both with the Diamond Collection), and others. Make a note of those gowns that appeal to you, and then visit a specialty bridal store or the bridal section of a major department store in your area. Virtually all wedding gowns are custom-ordered. When you've made your decision, the store orders the gown to the nearest size from the manufacturer—and it will arrive after six months or more. Fittings and alterations are done at the bridal store. Truly custom one-of-a-kind wedding gowns, often featuring rare lace, luxurious fabrics, and intricate details, are

made by only a few designers.

BRIDAL ACCESSORIES

Once the wedding gown is selected, complementary accessories such as the headpiece (usually made by the gown manufacturer or by a specialist at a bridal store) and shoes must be selected. These can usually be purchased through the bridal shop. However, if you've pur-

chased an extraordinary wedding gown, the shoes you wear with it should be equally extraordinary. The bridal shoes in the Peter Fox Shoe Collection are famed for their romantic, unusual designs. Shoes from Peter Fox are available through the company's mail-order catalogue and at the best shoe-stores nationwide; a store in New York City is devoted completely to the bridal collection.

Stunning lace and crochet wedding gowns designed by Lo of Lo New York, left, are made by hand in England.

No wedding gown is complete without a matching custom-made headpiece. This unique lace headpiece, above, was created by Lo New York.

Romantic boots and shoes are available from the "Reverie des Anges" bridal collection at Peter Fox Shoes, below.

COSMETICS

A stroll among the cosmetics counters in the average department store reveals a bewildering array of choices. Trying to select just the right shade of powder from among the dozens of color choices can reduce any executive woman to wavering indecision. Fortunately, a few prestigious cosmetics companies now offer custom blending services. This means that you can now get exactly the color you want in powder, foundation, blusher, eye shadow, lipstick. It also eliminates the possibility that a favorite shade of lipstick will be discontinued by the manufacturer just when you've used up the last of your supply. Companies offering custom blending include Charles of the Ritz, Prescriptives, and Visage Beauté. Although these lines are carried by most fine department stores, the custom service is available only at a select few.

Perhaps the ultimate in custom cosmetics is created by Elleance. This exclusive company offers nineteen incredibly rich lipstick shades enclosed in beautiful cases in a range of five spectacular designs. These limited-edition lipstick cases are made by hand from either 18-karat gold or sterling silver and adorned with precious gemstones. Each is numbered and signed; the silver cases can also be monogrammed. Should the available lipstick shades and case designs not be exactly what you want, Elleance technicians and craftspeople stand ready to custom-blend the color you desire and enclose it in a custom-made case.

Each gem-adorned, 18-karat gold octagonal lipstick case from Elleance, above, is signed and numbered as part of a very limited edition. The lipstick inside can be one of the nineteen exclusive Elleance shades, or it can be custom-blended especially for you.

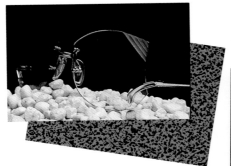

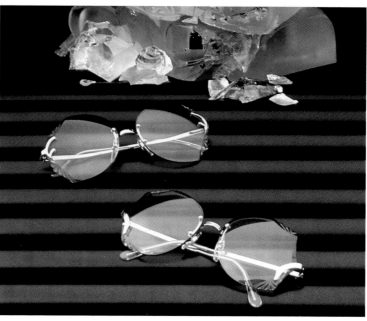

Genuinely stylish, original, and functional eyeglasses are surprisingly hard to find, even at the higher price levels. One of the few companies producing custom-made eyeglasses is Multi Facets. These sophisticated spectacles feature lenses hand cut to order with sculpted and beveled edges, including grooves, scallops, accent lines, diamond cuts, and tints. They can be adorned with your choice of precious or semi-precious stones. These lenses are completely functional. No matter what eyesight correction is needed (including bifocals and trifocals), the unique process used by Multi Facets results in lenses that are up to 50 percent thinner than conventional lenses—a feature particularly appreciated by very nearsighted people. The strikingly elegant frames are exceptionally strong and flexible, with a wide array of coatings and tints. Frames of 22-carat gold or sterling silver are also available.

Beautifully made gold frames, in styles ranging from traditional to

The unique back-bevel techniques used by Multi Facets to create custom-sculpted eyeglasses lenses, above and below, reduce the thick-ness of the lens by more than half. The lenses are attached to 22-karat gold electroplated French frames of unusual strength and flexibility.

ultramodern, are also available from Neostyle.

SUNGLASSES

Doctors recommend sunglasses for everyone to shield the eyes from excess UVA radiation outdoors. Make an entertaining and effective virtue of this necessity with sunglasses from Unex-SPECted. These unusual sunglasses feature individual, hand-painted miniature scenes marching across the top of the frame—water skiers, surfers, cowboys and Indians, Santa Claus, cows, and many other whimsical choices. No two pairs are exactly alike, and each pair is signed by the artist who designed it. Custom designs can also be ordered.

33

The *Notebook* umbrella, left, designed by Robert Venturi (better known for designing buildings), is silk-screened on cotton sateen. It is available through The Fabric Workshop in Philadelphia. Titled *Acid Rain*, the hand-painted cotton sateen umbrella, below, was made by Luis Cruz Araceta and exhibited at The Fabric Workshop.

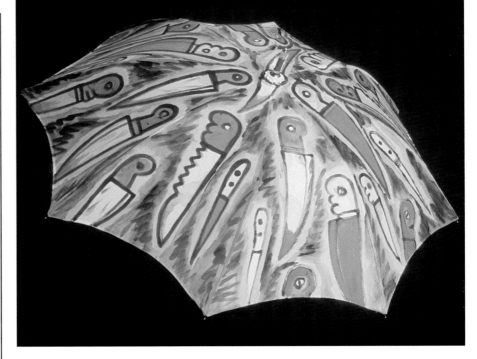

There are two schools of thought about umbrellas. One says that since an umbrella is likely to be lost, little should be invested in it. The other says that an umbrella, like any other personal accoutrement, should be functional, well-made, and attractive—and a good one is worth the investment.

The English, who live in a land of near-perpetual drizzle, know a lot about good umbrellas. The venerable London firm of Swaine Adeney Brigg and Sons Limited has refined the art of umbrella making to perfection. Holder of royal warrants to successive English monarchs since 1750, Swaine Adeney Brigg produces two basic types of umbrella: traditional and classic. The traditional type is produced by tapering a solid walking stick; a distinctive feature of this design is that the tips of the umbrella lie above the handle. In the classic design, the umbrella is assembled from a separate handle and stick; the tips fall below the shoulder of the handle, creating a slim, elegant appearance. Only the finest materials are used to create the Brigg umbrella. Runners, open caps and ferrules are made from solid brass; hand and top springs are individually fashioned from nickel silver. The variety of hand-formed wooden handles is extensive, and custom-made handles are also available. Skilled seamstresses create the cover from a wide choice of nylon fabrics, or in the best English black silk. Every cover is cut, sewn and tied securely to each rib, creating the classic domed shape that distinguishes the Brigg umbrella. Plated gold collars engraved with any design (a monogram or crest, for instance) can be fitted around the umbrella handle.

In addition to umbrellas, Swaine Adeney Brigg makes walking sticks of all sorts for men and women, country sticks, dress

sticks, and seat sticks. Specialty sticks available include those with silver thimble caps concealing scent sprayers, gas lighters, and glass vials; whiskey flask canes; .410 shotgun sticks covered in snakeskin; horsemeasure sticks; and, of course, custom-engraved sword sticks with sterling silver mounts.

Considerably less traditional are umbrellas designed by artists (including Robert Venturi) at The Fabric Workshop, a nonprofit institution devoted to fiber arts and based in Philadelphia. Imaginative, often whimsical, always water-resistant, these umbrellas are made of cotton canvas or cotton sateen. The designs are generally applied by silk-screening, sometimes combined with hand-painting, making each umbrella an individual work of art.

Umbrellas from Swaine Adeney Brigg & Sons Ltd., above, are made entirely by hand today much as they have been for the last 150 years. The firm was founded in 1750.

CHAPTER 2

ARCHITECTURAL HOME

HOUSES

A characteristic element of Deck House design, above, is the roof overhang, which keeps the house cooler in the summer, and warmer in the winter.

The decision to build a new house is never one to be made lightly, although it can also be one of the most rewarding experiences of a lifetime. It can mean a seemingly endless involvement with architects, engineers, contractors, and others, all in an effort to create exactly the house you want. One excellent way to get an outstanding, well-built house with a minimum of uncertainty and a maximum of convenience is to build it using the services of a nationally recognized custom home producer such as Timberpeg, Deck House, Northern Homes, Lindal Cedar Homes, or several others. These companies generally offer both standard and customized versions of their own distinctive component designs;

some will design the house from scratch. The houses tend toward airy contemporary looks using post-and-beam construction and a lot of wood and glass, although many traditional designs are also available. No matter what the design, the parts of the house are milled by the company and shipped to the building site, where they are assembled either by the client or by the client's contractor.

A great deal of thought goes into a custom home. The most important consideration is your budget. The house is only part of the total construction program. Site development, engineering, water and sewer connections, the foundation, and construction costs are

Houses from Timberpeg, above, are traditionally inspired but also thoroughly up-to-date. The design offers limitless creative flexibility in the arrangement of the interior spaces.

also major factors. Even so, building a component house can provide real savings and convenience. One great advantage is that these houses can be erected quickly. Depending on the size, the house can be framed, roofed, and fully weatherproofed within a month. This means that labor costs may be lower; interior work can also begin regardless of the season and be completed that much sooner.

38

Open floor plans, exposed beams and cathedral ceilings, and fine wood craftsmanship throughout are highlights of houses from Sawmill River Post & Beam, right.

The post-and-beam construction used by many component home companies allows great design flexibility, along with energy efficiency and easy maintenance. Buyers are strongly encouraged to participate in the design process—the best house design will depend on many individual factors, and no two clients have exactly the same needs. In addition, every building plot is different, and the design must be adjusted to take such factors as views and sun exposure into account. Another good reason for the client's active participation is that it is far, far easier and cheaper to make changes in the planning phase than in the field once construction has begun.

Once the preliminary sketches have been transformed into final plans, the client has two building options: do-it-yourself or hire a contractor (either an independent or someone affiliated with the house company). In either case, company representatives will work closely with you throughout the construction to answer questions and solve problems. The decision to do it yourself should be based on a rational assessment of your own abilities and time. However, even inexperienced people have had the enormous satisfaction of successfully building component houses by themselves (al-

though licensed subcontractors for the foundation and electrical, plumbing, and other work are necessary).

SELECTING A HOME BUILDER

Building a house is a huge investment of money, time, and emotion. Selecting the right component house for you is not a decision to be made lightly. One way to begin is to browse through home-design and architectural magazines. Clip out pictures of houses that appeal to you. At the same time, write to the component home manufacturers and ask for their literature. The designs offered by some are likely to please you more than

others. The next step is to contact the companies whose homes you like. The company will put you in touch with the local representative, who will probably be an architect or builder. Ask to see examples of the company's homes in your area. If possible, speak with the owners and ask them about their experience with the company. Ask the representative for references, and don't be embarrassed about checking them; and call your local Better Business Bureau as well. Bear in mind also that you will be working closely with the company representative, so it's important that there be good, open communication between you.

Architectual colorist Jill Pilaroscia specializes in advising the owners of Victorian homes on the best, most authentic colors for their houses. This building, right, is in San Francisco.

Architectural colorists specialize in selecting the colors for the interiors and exteriors of residential, commercial, and public buildings. The colors used in this complex, opposite page, were chosen by Jill Pilaroscia.

Do you suffer from anxiety every time you contemplate painting your house? Do you end up painting it white—again—simply because you can't think of anything better? Help is at hand, through the services of an experienced architectural colorist.

Not the sort of specialist found in every Yellow Pages, an architectural colorist offers professional consultations on the exterior and interior decoration of your house, particularly if it is an old one. Various periods of American architecture, with their typical building styles, are characterized by distinctly different palettes. The goal is to choose colors that are both congenial to the owner and appro-

priate to the period and architectural style of the house.

John Crosby Freeman is known as the Color Doctor. He explains the philosophy behind selecting house colors: "During the nineteenth century, painting a house was more than surface protection, more than presenting a fresh face toward the community. Exterior decoration was a conscious act of beautification in which color was used to enhance the meaning of a building

If a house call is impossible, Mr. Freeman usually asks the owner to send him photographs of the house along with a personal statement about the property. He listens to feelings, diagnoses

problems, and makes color recommendations designed to reveal the magic within an old building.

Jill Pilaroscia has worked as an architectural color consultant since 1975. Her goal is to select colors that respond to the architecture of a building and surrounding environment, including its site, structure, and ornamentation. The colors chosen are precisely matched to show off the structure and its ornaments to their greatest advantage and provide a coherent architectural statement. Pilaroscia works closely with her clients to find a creative formulation of color options that are both beautiful and appropriate.

The sharply con-
temporary, modu-
lar Gres kitchen,
opposite page,
above, designed by
Roberto Pamio and
distributed by IPI,
beautifully blends
functional details
with the aesthetics
of Italian design.

Decorative paint
effects combined
with traditional
English interiors
give the Venetian
kitchen from Small-
bone, right, its un-
conventional look.

The kitchen is often the hub of a busy home, the place where all family members seem to spend a lot of their time. The demands on this one room are huge: it must be efficient, attractive, safe, and versatile. The kitchen contains more elements—cabinets, appliances, fixtures, plumbing, wiring, and furniture—than any other room in the house. If ever custom design is called for, it's in the kitchen.

The fundamental design of a custom kitchen should revolve around what kitchen experts call the work triangle. This area is formed by the three major kitchen elements: range, refrigerator, and sink. More trips are made within this triangle than to any other areas of the kitchen. For the most efficient layout, kitchen designers recommend that the appliances be placed so that the distance between any two of them is no less than three feet and no more than seven feet, with the total of the triangle sides measuring no more than 22 feet or no less than 12 feet. A greater distance means unnecessary walking; a shorter one means cramped work space.

No matter how the kitchen is designed and organized, the cabinets are critical. Cabinets are to kitchens what furniture is to the other rooms of the house—an integral part of the total design. Custom cabinets built to your requirements will give you storage and work space that exactly meet your particular needs. The range of possible materials, sizes, finishes, hardware, colors, and special-feature units is vast.

A beautifully curved serving area in Italian walnut is a feature of the Venezia kitchen from IPI, opposite page, below. Other specialized custom features include built-in halogen lighting and an oversized cooking area with an integrated cylindrical hood and a striking lacquer finish.

THE CABINETMAKERS

The many outstanding companies providing custom cabinetry nationwide generally offer numerous

variations on all aspects of several different design groups. Beyond the standard dimensions, they also offer cabinets built to accommodate odd nooks and crannies, counters that are higher or lower than usual, cabinets built for special storage needs, and other solutions to specific problems.

Wood-Mode Cabinetry offers a combination of American raw materials and technology with the latest European look in cabinetry. In total, the company's traditional and European lines offer the consumer a varied choice of nearly twenty-five styles, thirty wood finishes, eighty different laminates, and five woods.

The Smallbone company, based in England, offers traditional English cabinetry in what is described as "unfitted" styles. This basically means that the kitchen combines freestanding and fixed units for maximum flexibility. Smallbone kitchens are designed for serious cooks. They incorporate a wealth of practical details—island units that com-

bine split-level chopping surfaces, a knife rack, a food-processor storage area, deep drawers and pull-out shelves, for example. Each Smallbone piece is handmade using only natural materials. The predominant wood is ash, either in its original colors, painted, or otherwise treated. A wide range of craft techniques is employed, including traditional cabinetmaking, cast metal work, and even basket-weaving.

Contemporary European designs are offered by two German firms, Poggenpohl and Allmilmö. Cabinets from these firms are strikingly modern, with sleek lines and bold colors.

Cooking and entertaining outdoors can be made much easier with custom outdoor entertainment centers from L'Oasis. These units consist of any combination of grill, wet bar, oven, refrigerator, microwave, and ice-maker into one free-standing cabinet. A wide choice of woods and counter tops is available, all designed to withstand the rigors of outdoor use.

The effective window and skylight design works beautifully with the light tones and sleek lines of the kitchen cabinetry, created by Wood-Mode, to brighten this kitchen, above.

Understated, traditionally styled kitchen cabinetry from Wood-Mode is easily adapted for less traditional uses, such as this open-design kitchen, opposite page.

THE DESIGNERS

Planning a new or renovated kitchen is a complex job involving a lot of variables. It's often best to have the advice of a qualified professional. A good source for this is the National Kitchen and Bath Association (NKBA). This nationwide, nonprofit organization offers a free listing of member firms— qualified professionals who design, supply, and install residential kitchens—and another directory listing certified kitchen designers. Both lists are organized by state and city to make selection easier.

A Louis XIV deck tub set from Phylrich International features hand-cut crystal and a swan spout, right.

The new Aventura unit from Kohler combines a circular shower with a whirlpool bath, below. It is available in a variety of high-fashion colors.

Baths and powder rooms used to be small, functional rooms on the low end of the design priority scale. No longer. Today's bath has become an elegant style center, often as an integrated part of the master suite. They're big, combining saunas, fitness equipment, and other high-tech accessories with all the traditional uses. They're also beautiful. White porcelain, plain tile, and stainless steel in the accustomed styles have been replaced by an incredible range of stunning new colors, materials, and designs. The custom look in luxury bathrooms is now easy to obtain.

Sherle Wagner has been taking bath furnishings far beyond plumbing since 1945. This famed firm virtually invented the concept of the luxury bathroom, and has led the way ever since. Custom work and limited editions are Sherle Wagner specialties. A typical piece might be a pedestal lavatory hand-carved from a single block of marble, with fittings made from gold, onyx, and semi-precious stones.

The extensive Kohler line of bath furnishings lives up to the company's guiding principle: beauty and practicality that endure. Kohler offers numerous custom options ranging from the contemporary to the nostalgic. An interesting major addition to the product line is the Artists Editions Program. These limited-edition fixtures and accessories are dec-orated with designs created by noted artists. Intended for those who wish to make a distinctive de-sign statement, the line includes coordinated lavatories, tiles, faucets, commodes, decorative ceramic containers, and other products.

Phylrich International was founded in 1959 with the goal of providing the ultimate in coordi-

A unique melding of Victorian flavor and modern flair, the Vintage Suite series from Kohler, above, offers a huge cast-iron tub that easily accommodates two. The Isis pattern, left, comes from the Kohler Artist Editions Reveries line of decorative lavatories.

nated luxury for the bath. The unique, handcrafted designs offered by this company are made by artisans from around the world. The emphasis is on combining European elegance with American expertise and quality. Phylrich concentrates on faucet sets, porcelain basins and tiles, and richly detailed wall accessories such as towel racks. The firm's products are available in numerous custom finishes and two-tone combinations.

Many companies that make custom kitchen cabinetry (see the section on kitchens on the preceding pages) also offer custom bathroom cabinetry. A good place to see a wide selection of bathroom furnishings, including the latest European imports, is a well-stocked home or bath center. However, for the best advice on a complex bath renovation or replacement, seek expert information from a qualified professional. To find a bathroom expert at no charge, contact the National Kitchen and Bath Association (see the kitchen section and Resources at the back of this book for more information).

Nothing says as much about yourself as the door you open to the world. It should complement and echo the architecture and detailing of your home; it should be sturdy and protective, but also expressive and welcoming. Surprisingly, doors are a neglected area of home design—the selection of standard doors at most well-stocked home centers is slim and undistinguished. For unique doors that make a statement, a custom designer is needed, someone who combines artistic ability with craft skills.

Each door created in Al Garvey's studio at Door/Ways is expressly designed for the individual client. A unique combination of design, materials, color, and finish contributes to the elegance of every door. The large variety of possibilities includes contemporary textured or faux finishes; exotic hardwoods; all forms of stained, etched, and leaded glass; and metal work, including custom-designed knobs and levers. All Garvey's doors are beautifully made using frame and panel construction, with mortise and tenon joints throughout.

Raised-panel wooden doors from David Mulder are custom-built by hand to highlight any room or entrance. They are also avail-

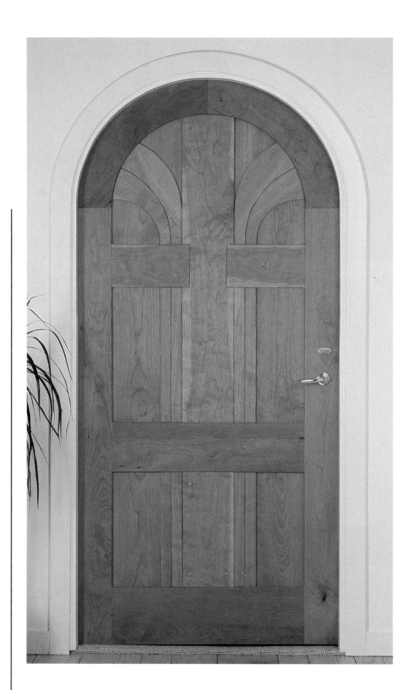

Doors crafted by Al Garvey, above, reflect the architectural and design elements of the setting.

48

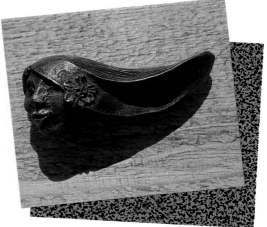

Glass artist Anne Sutherland and her husband, furniture designer Tim Sutherland, gave antique walnut entry doors, left, new carved-glass panels and restored them. Bronze lever door handles and other architectural details are made to order by architect William Hubartt. Below is the Orchid Wave design.

able as bi-fold and cabinet doors; the thickness of the wood and the number of panels can be matched to individual specific design requirements.

Any door can be given distinction if the ordinary hardware is replaced with something special. Custom-made door levers and other accessories are available from architect William Hubartt of Architectural Bronzes. These handsome pieces of functioning art range from the serious to the whimsical.

49

Founded in metalworking disciplines, Paley Studios produces a wide range of architectural ornamentation. The gates at the top of this page are made of forged steel.

The DeKoven Forge specializes in custom iron and metalwork. This detail, above, is from a grille in a wooden gate; the metals are forged steel, copper, and brass.

These intricately detailed, award-winning gates, opposite page, were designed and built by ironworker Robert Ponsler of Wonderland Products.

GATES

The gates leading into your property also make a statement about you. Standard metal gates are often ordinary if not actually forbidding in their design. Custom gates designed for a particular environment are sensitive to their surroundings—they can be both protective and welcoming.

The traditional blacksmithing skills required to create artistic gates, grilles, fences, railings, and other architectural metalwork are still practiced at a number of forges around the country. By definition, the work these talented craftspeople do is all individually designed and created.

Machin Designs USA creates conservatories along elegantly traditional lines, left. Sunrooms from Lindal, opposite page, are framed in western red cedar, not metal, for beauty and energy efficiency.

SUNROOMS

Letting light into your home through the addition of a sunroom (also called a solarium or conservatory) can be a great solution to a number of design needs. Dark houses can be opened up by sunrooms installed around an inside corner, or by installing sun dormers on the second story. Sun dormers also help create dramatic entrance areas. Some prefer to add a sun-filled breakfast nook, while others prefer a wide-open great room for entertaining. Sunrooms can enclose a hot tub, adding a sense of open space to that relaxing experience; small swimming pools can also be enclosed in sunrooms. A sunroom can also rescue a neglected area of a house—by enclosing an underutilized deck, for example, you can make it into a favorite year-round spot.

The sunroom is a room for all seasons. State-of-the-art glazing combined with shading and ventilation systems keep the rooms from overheating in the summer; passive solar designs can actually help heat the rest of the house in the winter.

Sunrooms from Lindal Cedar SunRooms come in two attractive architectural styles with numerous custom variations to fit virtually any size or shape. Every sunroom is carefully customized by the company for the site where it will be installed. A skilled person with a helper or two can assemble a typical Lindal sunroom on its foundation in just a few days. This is because the parts are delivered labeled, cut, drilled, and notched for easy, fast installation.

Solar rooms from Janco can be adapted to many handsome and unusual uses. These custom-designed solariums incorporate a tubular framing system, integral condensation control, concealed connectors, and a wide variety of glazing systems. Janco products are designed and installed by a national network of dealers.

The design heritage of Amdega Conservatories goes back to 1874, when sunrooms were in their original Victorian heyday. This English firm still makes conservatories in traditional period styles, but the firm's engineers use modern construction and glazing techniques. Amdega offers custom designs, and often works closely with clients' architects.

GREENHOUSES

The dream of every dedicated gardener is a greenhouse, allowing plants, flowers, and vegetables to grow year-round without regard to the weather. Detached greenhouses are expensive, inconvenient, and often not particularly attractive. Happily, modern design offers a solution: lean-to greenhouses that are built onto one wall of the existing house. These greenhouses add beauty and space to the home, and have the additional advantages of ease of installation and substantial cost savings. In addition, they can be custom-designed to fit special needs such as unusual sizes or connecting to outside overhangs and porches.

Greenhouses from Janco are available in many different models. Janco offers insulated lean-to designs that combine the energy efficiency of insulated glass with the economy and style selection of traditional single-glazed greenhouses. All Janco greenhouses are available with full-length roof vents to provide the air circulation vital to healthy plants.

SWIMMING POOLS

An elegant pool, right, was designed by Watts Pool Company of Houston, Texas. The pool has a hydrotherapy area, built-in wall seats, and a diving area; it is surrounded by 2,000 square feet of deck space.

The days when all in-ground swimming pools were the same rectangular shape, with the occasional exception of a kidney-shaped pool for the daring, are long past. Using modern construction technology, pools today can be built in virtually any configuration desired. In addition, they can now be built in places where pools were once unimaginable: on steep slopes, in limited spaces, on irregularly shaped lots, around existing landscaping and natural features, and almost anywhere space permits.

When planning a pool, the selection of a dealer is critical. Look for a dealer who is a member of the National Spa and Pool Institute. There are more than 3,900 members of the NSPI in more than 70 local chapters. Membership means the dealer is professionally committed to stringent standards of fair business practices, safety, superior product quality, and service integrity.

This freeform swimming pool, opposite page, below, was created by Aquarius Pools of Sacramento, California. The natural-looking design is beautifully integrated with the landscaping; the area of water surface is 1,350 square feet. Covered or enclosed pools for year-round use in colder climates are becoming increasingly popular. New ideas in pool design allow virtually any requirement to be met, as shown by this innovative covered pool in Michigan, right.

Some dealers can provide both the swimming pool and the landscaping to go with it. However, many clients prefer to work with both a landscape architect and a dealer to get an outstanding pool. As with any major construction project, ask for quotes and references from a few different dealers. The final contract should be very specific, with such information as: approximate start and completion dates (with appropriate allowances for delays); specifications for size, shape, and equipment; understandings regarding unexpected costs such as hitting solid rock during the excavation; a schedule of payments; and a description of aftercare service.

An in-ground swimming pool offers the most options in design and appearance, and has the additional advantage of being a very durable structure. All local building and zoning codes should be checked before construction begins; because in-ground pools are generally considered an addition to property value, local authorities may reappraise your home.

Once the pool has been designed and the excavation made, steel reinforcing rods are installed. The actual pool is then made using either gunite or shotcrete. With both methods, a concrete mixture consisting of sand and cement is air-sprayed through the nozzle of a hose. It is then finished with a fine coat of plaster. The pool's thick shell helps it withstand frost pressure in cooler climates, and it rarely requires any structural repairs.

55

CHAPTER 3
HOME FURNISHINGS

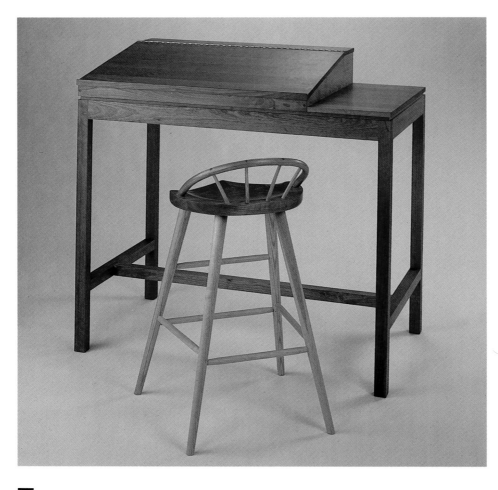

Handcrafted furniture from Thomas Moser offers elegant simplicity, as demonstrated by this high standing desk and bowback, 31-inch stool, left. The desk shown here is designed for right-handed users; a reversed version can be made for left-handers. Artist/furniture maker Timothy Sutherland creates signature works, opposite page, utilizing fine woods and impeccable joinery. This cabinet is a typical example.

There are a lot of good reasons for wanting custom-made furniture, but the primary one is quality. In a way that no factory-made furniture can, custom-made furniture combines impeccable craftsmanship and an artist's unique vision.

As a rule custom-made furniture is conservative in design. This does not mean that the crafts-people work only in traditional styles. Rather, it means that these artisans build their furniture to last. The pieces are carefully hand-built and finished using only the finest materials. The designs are often contemporary, but they are never trendy.

Every furniture maker has an individual style, but most will welcome input from the client. Show the designer pictures of similar pieces you admire, and try to explain exactly what it is you want— even crude sketches will help. The exact dimensions of the piece and the room in which it will be should always be specified by the client and discussed with the artist; otherwise, there is a real danger that a custom-made piece will be ill-proportioned for the room or purpose, or might not even fit through the door. It's also a good idea to specify a firm budget, bearing in mind that shipping expenses are generally charged to the client.

Remember that rare woods or unusual materials will affect the price accordingly.

The design (from the customer's specifications), approval, construction, and finishing of custom furniture takes time, often a long time. It can take weeks of hand labor, for example, to give wooden furniture a satiny hand-rubbed finish. Furniture this well made should be treated with care and respect. Place it where it can be admired and used, but avoid placing it in direct sunlight or near a radiator or air conditioner. Extremes of temperature and humidity are bad for all furniture, particularly wooden pieces. To keep

casting are often produced in limited editions, with the mold destroyed after the last piece is made. Bronze, because it is strong enough to stand alone yet supple enough to be shaped with delicate details, is a favorite metal among furniture artists. The work of Ilana Goor provides some excellent examples. Among stone workers, Paul Puccio is noted for his exquisite furniture, particularly tables. Each Puccio piece is handcrafted from marble, granite, or onyx selected for the richness of its grain and the diversity of its pattern and color. Individual pieces are signed and numbered by the artist.

Custom-made brass beds are available from Isabel Brass Furniture. These beds are made from heavy-walled solid brass tubing adorned with solid brass castings. In addition to fine construction and custom design, Isabel brass beds are distinguished by their integrated frames. The frame keeps the bed from skidding, rattling, and squeaking; it can be made for a mattress of any size and height.

Excellent design, innovative solutions to functional challenges, and meticulous joinery are all found in the work of Ed Wohl. This high chair, left, is crafted in cherry with a removable tray.

Trained in traditional cabinetry and restoration techniques, Glenn de Gruy builds custom furniture; this child's four-poster crib/bed, below, is designed to last.

Heirloom-quality hand-painted children's furniture is offered by Thank Heavens for Little Ones, opposite page. Each piece is prepared by an artist and covered with several coats of sealer for easy cleaning. The furniture can be personalized with the child's name.

FURNITURE FOR CHILDREN

Custom-made furniture for children tends to fall into two categories: hand-painted and heirloom. In the hand-painted area, the firm of Boston & Winthrop stands out. In addition to standard designs that are custom-painted to match the decor of the child's room, the firm offers delightful specialties such as canopied poster beds.

Custom-made, handcrafted cradles, high chairs, and the like are all designed to be passed down to future generations. When commissioning these pieces, keep in mind the safety guidelines of the U.S. Consumer Product Safety Commission. High chairs should have a sturdy frame, good balance and stability, and a restraining device to secure the baby to the chair seat; the tray should stay in position once it is properly locked. There should be no holes or openings that can catch fingers, toes or buttons. Safety requirements for cribs and cradles are quite stringent. The slats must be spaced no more than 2⅜ inches apart. The mattress must fit snugly—there should be no more than the width of two adult fingers between the mattress edge and the side of the crib. If you must have corner posts, they should be no higher than ⅝ of an inch to prevent entanglement; there should be no cutouts in the head- and footboards that could entrap the child's head. Of course, the crib or cradle should be solidly built and very stable.

A floor custom-designed by Randy Yost is installed in an elaborate hall, below. Floors from Yost & Co. often combine several exotic woods with metal, ceramic, or even semiprecious stone.

Leaving aside the question of kitchen floors (a subject for another book in itself), most custom floors are created for the public areas of a home: the entryway, living room, and dining room. The most traditional floor covering is hardwood laid down in classic patterns or simple planks; borders can be added to define a specific area or just to add an additional decorative touch. The warmth, elegance, and durability of hardwood floors make them perpetually popular.

Floors made by Kentucky Wood Floors grace the Oval Office and East Room of the White House, but the bulk of the firm's business is with private residential customers. More than three dozen patterns in a variety of finishes are available in addition to custom designs. Kentucky Wood Floors can also provide matching custom millwork, including baseboards, moldings, stair and handrail systems, and the like.

Randy Yost of Yost & Co. creates distinctive, one-of-a-kind floors that combine exotic hard-woods with other materials, including mother-of-pearl, bronze, granite, and even malachite and lapis lazuli. Yost's floors are extremely beautiful and often extremely complex—one design used 46,000 pieces.

If a hardwood floor isn't suitable or isn't what you want, several creative alternatives using paint are possible. Painted floors were common in Colonial America, in part because the hand labor needed to sand and finish coarse

Tromploy Inc. is a cooperative of fine artists who have mastered the art of decorative painting. They specialize in faux finishes and painted illusions, such as this faux marble foyer, below.

The old-fashioned techniques of stenciling and painting floors are popular again. Randy Jones of Decorative Arts Ltd. created and painted this floor design, right, on over 900 feet of a new addition to an old house.

and imperfect floorboards was out of the question. Today painted floors are popular again. They are still sometimes used to cover flaws, but more often the painting is strictly decorative. Stenciling, an American folk-art tradition that flourished from the late 1700s until the 1840s, is also becoming popular again, particularly for use in period houses. Another early American folk-art form is the painted floor cloth. Designs resembling those in far more costly rugs and carpets were painted and stenciled on durable sailcloth. The concept has enjoyed a resurgence today. Interestingly, the designs tend to be much more contemporary than those created for modern-day painted or stenciled floors.

Numerous artists create innovative custom painted and stenciled floors and floor cloths today. Among them are Lynn Goodpasture, Leslie Ann Powers, Rinder's New York Flooring, Patricia Dreher, Evergreene Painting Studio, and Decorative Arts Limited.

65

The plain white walls favored for the past few decades are giving way today to painted surfaces decorated with an exciting variety of techniques: stippling, marbling, graining, glazing, rag-rolling, stenciling, faux finishes, trompe l'oeil effects, hand-painted wallpapers, and more. These intriguing finishes are artis-tically pleasing and also practical. Paint in its many manifestations can be a resourceful solution to decorating problems that would otherwise require structural changes. Low ceilings, small rooms, uneven or rough walls, unsightly cornices, strange angles, dead spaces, funny nooks, windowless rooms, and many other structural peculiarities can be all improved upon with paint and imagination. Painted finishes can also be surprisingly durable once they are varnished.

Numerous talented artists can create custom-designed wall treatments. Selecting the right artist can be very time-consuming, because you will want to see each

artist's portfolio and discuss your ideas. Working through an interior designer who is familiar both with you and with the artists in your area could be a big help.

When it comes to surfaces, most artists aren't all that fussy. The same artists who paint your walls can also be asked to decorate ceilings, floors, doors, baseboards, even furniture.

WALLPAPER

In the days when the aristocracy lived in drafty palaces, costly tapestries hung on the walls as much to help keep the room warm as to decorate it. By the seventeenth century, lesser ranks were putting painted paper and fabric on the walls of their houses in imitation of tapestries. By the end of the eighteenth century, no properly decorated house was without elaborate wallpaper; by the end of the nineteenth century, wallpaper was even more popular, helped along by printing advances that allowed more color and detail. Nearing the end of the twentieth century, wallpaper is still very much in style. Hand-painted wallpapers are particularly interesting for those seeking the custom look. The patterns and textures of these wallpapers can be created to order. Because even standard designs are done by hand, every piece is unique.

PANELING

Wood paneling gives traditionally designed rooms, particularly dens, libraries, and formal living and dining rooms, a wonderful rich glow. The quiet warmth of a paneled room makes it a distinctive setting for fine furnishings

and art. Rodger Reid has been considered one of the best craftsmen in the field for over twenty years. His beautifully handcrafted paneling is made from the finest hardwoods, hand-rubbed with oil and then waxed to bring out the natural beauty of the woods.

67

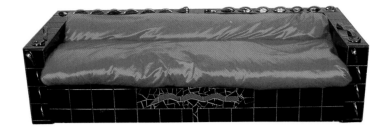

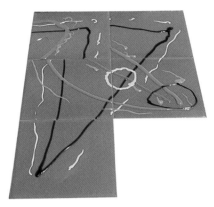

Ceramic tile was once an important part of exterior and interior design, as can be seen, for example, in the decoration of many Beaux Arts buildings from the late nineteenth century. The increased use of glass and steel, starting in the 1930s, sharply reduced the use of decorative tiles. Today handcrafted, original tile is returning to interior design schemes as a durable, versatile, and beautiful way of adding color and texture. Tiles can be used as the primary surface for floors, walls, countertops, and more—or they can simply be decorative accents.

A number of studios are providing the materials for the comeback of ceramic tile. The artists working in tile offer a number of intriguing options. Traditional square tiles can be made with flat or textured surfaces using a variety of glazes. Custom designs can be painted on the tiles, and tiles in complementary colors or with custom-painted accents can be made. Custom-designed murals painted in tile are another popular technique, particularly attractive on kitchen walls. Natural variations in colors and glazes mean that every handpainted ceramic tile is an individual work; no two are exactly alike, even when the same design is repeated.

Another option is shaped tiles, used to create interesting designs and ceramic mosaics, particularly for floors and walls. Again, the colors, textures, and glazes are created to order.

Flat tiles, either glazed or un-

Ceramic artist Nina Yankowitz creates unusual glazed tile designs, left. As her unique tiled sofa, above, demonstrates, tiles are not just for floors and walls. The artists at Architectural Ceramics created this imaginative bathtub surround, below.

At Starbuck Goldner Studios the emphasis is on handmade ceramic tiles for original patterns, opposite page. Reproduction work for restorations is another specialty.

glazed, can be used on any surface. Relief tiles, where the surface has been embossed with a textured design, are better suited for low-traffic areas such as backsplashes, walls, borders, and friezes. Relief tiles are usually finished with just a single glaze to bring out the pattern. In addition to creating the decorative tiles, ceramics studios offer matching finishing pieces such as mouldings and borders.

Generally at least four weeks are needed to make a ceramic tile, dry it, fire it, paint and glaze it, and fire it again. Allow plenty of time when placing your order. Tile prices are calculated by the square foot, and they can vary greatly depending on the complexity of the design. Provide the tilemaker with accurate measurements of the area to be tiled. Sam-

ples showing the colors and textures of the other surfaces in the area (the floor, counters, walls and so on) are also helpful.

Installing fine ceramic tiles re- quires an expert's touch, since the surface must be carefully pre- pared. To find a competent tile set- ter, check your local Yellow Pages or ask a reliable contractor for a referral. Don't attempt to set ex- pensive custom-made tiles your- self—if you make a mistake, you will probably have to break the tile to remove it.

LIGHTING

Every lamp from Stuber/Stone is signed by the artist; custom orders are welcome, right.

"Light is the first of painters," said American philosopher Ralph Waldo Emerson. This is a statement taken seriously by interior designers, who know that proper lighting is an integral part of a good room design. Getting that proper lighting can be difficult, however, particularly when what is needed must be not only functional but striking. All too often, despite the vast array of lamps available from manufacturers, original design and fine craftsmanship are difficult to find. However, a number of designers today are creating custom-made and one-of-a-kind lighting designs in a variety of beautiful and practical ways.

THE DESIGNERS

70

Porcelain, in its many manifestations, is a favorite medium for lighting designs because of its translucent properties. Among the creative artists working with porcelain are Curtis and Suzan Benzlé of Benzlé Porcelain. Their columnar lights are made with porcelain squares framed in aluminum with a Plexiglas core.

Lamps from Gemma Studios have shades made of glass and bronze, and bases of porcelain and bronze.

At Stuber/Stone, the lamps are hand cast in a gypsum plaster aggregate, an alabasterlike substance resembling polished stone or fine fired clay. The shades are made of handmade paper. A unique ceramic casting formula is used by Janna Ugone to make contemporary lamps and wall sconces showing a strong sculptural and geometric influence. Robert McCandless constructs custom and limited-edition lamps and wall sconces from a wide range of materials, including sandblasted glass.

Glass, the most traditional of lamp materials, is also one of the most modern. Noel and Janene Hilliard at Lamps by Hilliard use heat-formed glass and cast bronze to make their custom-crafted table lamps, sconces, and floor lamps. Unusual table lamps made of hand-blown glass tiles held together with a network of metal solder are also made. At Glasslight, Joel Bless makes beautiful lamps of all sorts using free-blown glass. Joe Clearman at Clearman Art Glass also works in free-blown glass, using no assistants and no molds. Cathy Richardson at Nature's Image Studio uses stained glass techniques to make sculptural lighting.

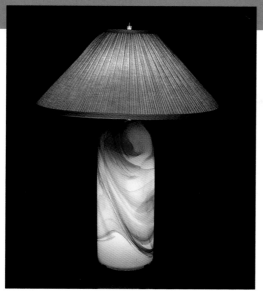

This unique cylinder lamp from Glasslight, left, has a free-blown base with swirled glass colors cased in clear glass.

Wall sconces produced by Benzle Porcelain, left, are made of translucent porcelain framed in aluminum.

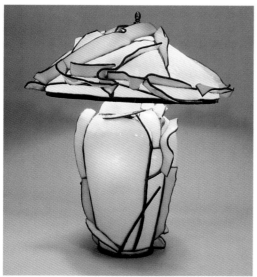

Contemporary, limited-edition lighting from Lamps by Hilliard often incorporates heat-formed glass, left.

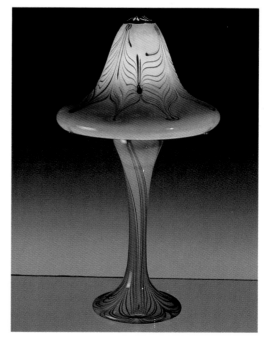

At Clearman Art Glass the lamps are free-blown by glass artist Joe Clearman, without the use of molds or assistance, left.

Robert McCandless produced this Tri-cone lamp, left, in a limited edition of fifty.

Glass nuggets, left, add highlights to this cylindrical stained-glass lamp from Cathy Richardson at Nature's Image Studio.

Stylish and functional, these colorful tabletop torchieres, above, from Janna Ugone are available in a wide range of colors and surfaces. A free-blown glass shade with tiger stripes of powdered glass cased in clear glass adorns this floor lamp from Glasslight, right. The texture-painted metal pole has a granite base.

72

SPECIALIZED LIGHTING

The selection of a proper light source is particularly critical when collections of art, antiques, or furniture are an important part of an interior setting. The right light can enhance the art while providing an inviting setting or relaxed mood.

Wendelighting has been illuminating art collections and gardens—including those at the Louvre, the Vatican, and the White House—for over fifty years. The company offers optical framing projectors for lighting art objects. These can be recessed into the ceiling for concealment, or they can be mounted on a track or surface. For shelf or cabinet displays, Wendelighting offers systems featuring miniature lamps with exceptional illumination. Optical projectors and walk reflectors for outdoor lighting are also available.

Handcrafted,
etched copper or
brass switch plates
and dimmers,
above, are made
by Kevin Loughran
of House Jewelry.
Each piece is
unique, and custom
orders are
welcome.

LIGHTING RESTORATION

Historically correct lighting is critical to an authentic architectural restoration. Restoring a valuable antique light fixture is not a job for an amateur, however. To clean the light, restore any lost or damaged parts, replace old wiring, and adapt the unit for modern use requires an expert. One of the world's leading specialists in lighting in general, and lighting restoration in particular, is Viggo Rambusch, head of Rambusch Studios in New York City. Founded in 1898, Rambusch Studios has won four Lumen Awards, the lighting industry's equivalent of the Oscar. Today the firm specializes in restoration and replication work.

LIGHTING ACCESSORIES

If your design scheme calls for lamp shades in the same fabric as your couch, it also calls for custom work. Ruth Vitow of Ruth Vitow Custom Lamps and Shades in New York City is a legend in the lighting business; she's been at it for more than forty-five years. Another source of custom shades in New York is Abat-Jours. In California Sue Johnson makes Victorian-style lamp shades and lamps.

Why turn on an extraordinary lamp with an ordinary switch? Kevin Loughran of House Jewelry produces unusual, one-of-a-kind switch plates and light dimmers made of etched nickel on copper or brass.

73

CHAPTER 4
CRAFTSPEOPLE

Textile artist Beth Minear created this boldly patterned rug, right, called *Razzamatazz Jazz*. It measures 51 × 91 inches.

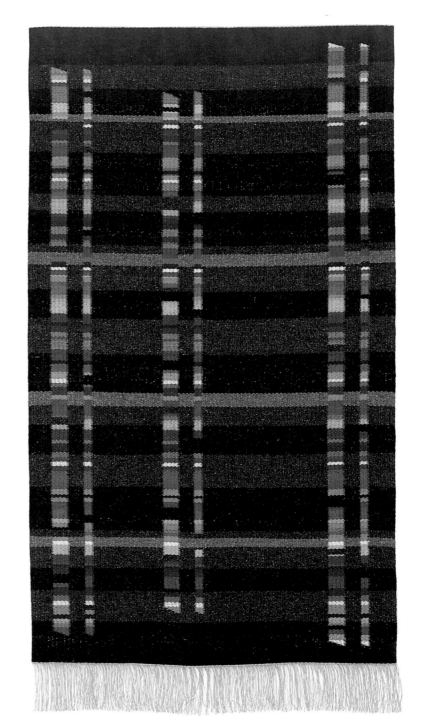

In Colonial times, every household had a well-used spinning wheel. Using natural substances such as goldenrod blossoms and butternut bark, the Colonial housewife dyed her own wool and flax, spun it into yarn and often wove her own cloth. To keep the chill off her floors, she used rugs woven directly from heavy yarn.

Continuing a long American tradition of innovative rug-making, contemporary fiber artists often dye their own yarns. They continue to use wool, but they also use cotton and other natural yarns, sometimes combined with rayon and other synthetic fibers. Their dyes are more vivid and long lasting, and the range of colors is almost infinite. Today's rug makers work in a variety of eclectic and individual styles that often incorporate regional or international influences, and they use modern looms that allow unusual sizes and techniques.

A custom rug can be an expensive proposition, easily costing as much as a good antique Oriental rug. Generally the rug

Ikat is a Japanese dying technique that imparts a subtle pattern to the wool skeins. Rug artist Lyn Sterling Montagne used ikat for the custom-woven rug shown, right. Rug designer Terry Mertz specializes in unusual custom work. This rug, below, incorporates a family coat of arms.

maker charges by the square foot, taking into account such factors as custom dyeing, the difficulty of execution, unusual dimensions, and so on. There are significant advantages to custom rugs. The colors, patterns, and textures can be made exactly to your needs, but more importantly, the size and shape of the rug can be specified. This is particularly useful to those who want rugs for spaces with unusual shapes. Motifs and patterns with particular meaning to the client, or that coordinate with other furnishings, can also be part of a custom rug.

Modern rugs are durable. Most do not need the delicate handling required by valuable antique rugs, and thus can endure being used in an active household. Even so, some care must be taken to keep a custom rug in good condition. The piece should be kept away from direct sunlight to keep the colors from fading and the fibers from breaking down. Regular vacuuming removes dust and soil buildup; have the rug dry cleaned by an experienced professional occasionally. Air the rug on both sides every few weeks, and check every now and then for possible insect and moth damage. If the rug is stained or damaged, contact the artist—repairs can often be made. Many rug artists confess to some ambivalence about seeing their work walked upon. If you decide that your custom rug is too beautiful to be covered by furniture or slept on by the dog, it can be displayed as a dramatic wall hanging instead.

The traditional Blazing Star pattern is the basis for this colorful, king-size quilt, right, by Judy Freeman.

In the late 1700s thrifty and resourceful American housewives invented the patchwork quilt. Precious scraps of fabric were saved and carefully pieced together into attractive, functional coverlets, often at quilting "bees," where a group of women (preferably eight) gathered to sew the blocks together. By the 1850s patchwork quilts became such works of art that they sometimes took years to create and were no longer used as coverlets. Rather, they were kept as heirlooms, one reason that many well-preserved quilts from the period survive today as coveted items for collectors of folk art.

Although the rapid spread of manufactured goods after the Civil War led to a sharp decline in quilting, among fiber artists today there is renewed interest in a form that is fundamentally simple and honest. Some artists work along traditional lines, inspired by Amish and Mennonite designs and producing variations on classic patterns such as Log Cabin, Lone Star, and Star of Bethlehem. Many others have brought quilting into the modern age with sharply contemporary designs.

Whether the design is traditional or modern, a custom-made quilt will always be a treasured possession. The amount of hand work in each quilt will vary depending on the artist, but every custom quilt is unique. Quilts can be made to whatever size is desired, using colors, fabrics, and stuffings (down or synthetic) that meet whatever requirements necessary. In a simply furnished room, a custom quilt on the bed or hanging on the wall can provide the needed panache to make the room special.

If the quilt is designed to be used as bed cover, the size of the quilt should be larger than the size of the bedsheets. Depending on the height of the bed, its headboards and footboards (if any), the amount of overhang desired and any other special factors, a queen-size quilt might work perfectly well on a smaller bed—or vice versa. In general, however, these quilt dimensions are approximately accurate for different bed sizes: crib, 40 × 60 inches; cot, 65 × 108 inches; twin, 74 × 108 inches; full, 94 × 106 inches; queen, 100 × 112 inches; king, 106 × 112 inches.

Commissioned as a
wedding present,
this colorfully con-
temporary quilt,
above, by Jean
Hoblitzell is called
Coming Together.

The right sort of pillows scattered invitingly on a couch can be just what a room needs to tie the design together. To get just the pillow needed, in just the right size, colors and pattern, may mean having it custom made—a surprisingly easy solution.

Marjorie Lawrence, owner of The Pillowry, is well known in the interior design world for her extensive knowledge of textiles. Working with her vast collection of fabric fragments (including many hard-to-get antique textiles), trims, and backing fabrics, she can create pillows that exactly match and complement the environment. Interestingly, custom pillows from The Pillowry cost no more than stock pillows, but they take longer to make.

Cynthia Winika creates pillows she calls "fat pictures." Definitely meant to be used, these pillows have designs created by a combination of silk-screening, etching, and hand-painting with acrylics. Her monoprint pillows on silk charmeuse are one-of-a-kind creations done by creating the original image on a zinc or Plexiglas plate using brushes and inked rollers. The image is transferred to the silk from the plate under pressure from an etching press.

Hand-painted pillows, scarves, and other fabrics from Marliss Jensen use rich, vibrant dyes applied to silk crepe de chine, above, left. Leather pillows in vivid colors are made by Sondra Sardis, above, center and right. A piece from an antique tapestry is turned into an amusing pillow by Marjorie Lawrence of The Pillowry, left.

Marjorie Lawrence of The Pillowry custom-designs pillows using fragments of old, rare, and unusual fabrics from around the world, above. Doris Louie uses her skills as a rug weaver to create pillows that incorporate the patterns and colors of the American Southwest, right.

A fine concert grand piano consists of thousands of pieces, all fitted together with consummate artistry to make a unique musical instrument. Good pianos are made by hundreds of reputable manufacturers all over the world, but by universal acclamation the very best pianos are made by Steinway & Sons of New York City.

The Steinway story begins in 1853, when Heinrich Engelhard Steinway founded his piano company. Pianos made by Steinway and his sons quickly became favorites, and the firm prospered. To this day, building a nine-foot concert grand Steinway Model D takes some twelve thousand individual pieces, some two hundred workers, and nearly two years. Some automated machinery is used, but basically the complicated process of building a Steinway is done by hand, carefully and patiently. The final step of voicing the piano can take twenty-five hours. In this process, a craftsman called a tone regulator makes the piano *sound* like a Steinway by skillfully making min-

ute adjustments to the action, giving the piano the richness of tone and range that characterize a Steinway piano. Somewhere in the construction process each Steinway begins to take on its own personality; the voicing completes the process.

About 3,400 Steinway pianos are built every year at the company's plant in Long Island City; another 1,800 or so are made at the branch factory in Hamburg, Germany. In 1988 Steinway & Sons built its 500,000th piano. Piano number 100,000, built in 1903, was installed in Theodore Roosevelt's White House; piano number 300,000 was presented to the White House under Franklin Roosevelt's administration. Both pianos are now in the permanent collections of the Smithsonian Institution, where they have been declared National Artifacts.

The case of piano 500,000 is inscribed with the laser-etched signatures of the eight hundred living Steinway artists, who together represent 90 percent of the pianists performing with major

Every Steinway grand piano, above, is carefully built and individu- **ally numbered; some 12,000 pieces go into its construction.**

symphony orchestras today. Piano number 500,000 will tour the world for two years and then be sold at an auction to benefit the Steinway Foundation for pianists and composers.

Steinway pianos set the world standard for how a piano should look, play, and sound. They are timeless heirlooms, and they are also excellent investments. Steinway pianos are routinely resold for more than twice their original cost; the older the piano, the more valuable it becomes.

If you can't have a Steinway Model D, the next-best thing would be a Bösendorfer Imperial, at six inches over nine feet. Bösendorfer pianos are made in limited numbers: since the firm's founding in 1828, just over 40,000 pianos, or about 250 a year, have been made, entirely by hand.

Bösendorfer grand pianos, left, are crafted in a converted monastery in Vienna. Only about a hundred are exported to the United States every year.

The complex job of bending the wood to make the rim of a Steinway piano requires six highly skilled, very strong workers, below. The rim will spend ten weeks in a humidity-controlled room before being sent on for the next step in production.

BOOKBINDERS

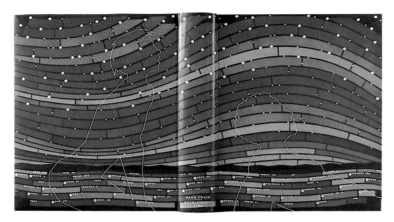

Michael Wilcox used navy blue goatskin, colored leathers, and gold and silver tooling for this binding of *The Adventures of Huckleberry Finn*,

left. An evocation of writer Honoré de Balzac in the cubist style of painter Pablo Picasso adorns this bookbinding by Silvia Rennie, below.

The art of the bookbinder is a noble and ancient one that today combines the best of past traditions and present craftsmanship. Bookbinders must be concerned with the entire structure of the book, since the binding must protect as well as adorn the book. When rebinding an old volume, this could mean cleaning, mending, and sometimes deacidifying the paper before binding can begin. The actual binding is a complex process employing a wide range of materials. Among those used are many kinds of papers (including Japanese tissues, handmade papers, and special acid-free buffered papers); various binders' boards and cards; cords and threads made of linen, hemp, or silk; the finest goatskin and calfskin leathers; gold and silver leaf; adhesives of various kinds; and numerous coloring agents, oils, and waxes. In addition, the flyleaves and insides of the covers may be lined with mar-

bled paper or silk, and a cloth-covered box with a soft lining of felt, velvet, or padded silk may be made to protect the binding.

A fine binding can take weeks to design and execute, and the best bookbinders have waiting lists that extend for years. However, when the book is important, the binding should be too. Tattered heirloom volumes such as family Bibles deserve rebinding as much to preserve them as to honor them. Book collectors, especially those who purchase fine

editions illustrated with original prints, often commission creative bindings. Private collectors, dealers, and libraries also commission more traditional, highly finished, gold-tooled bindings. And of course, any special book (your own, for example) can have a special binding created for it.

A surprisingly large number of artists work in bookbinding and related crafts (making portfolios to hold prints, for example). The work illustrated on these pages is just a sampling drawn from members of the Guild of Book Workers; other organizations, such as the Center for Book Arts or the Minnesota Center for Book Arts, sponsor artists and offer courses. Exhibitions of private-press books and fine bindings are often held at art museums and libraries, and the many antiquarian book shows held around the country every year are a good place to see (and purchase) outstanding examples of the binder's art.

A detail, right, from Frank Mowery's magnificent binding of *Amazon Parrots* shows the "feathers" made from hundreds of cut, dyed, and shaped pieces of leather. The beak and eye are painted vellum.

Alum-tawed pigskin surrounds two stunning inset panels in a binding, left, designed by Frank Mowery for *Amazon Parrots*, an illustrated atlas of all the known species of parrots from that region.

A portrait of yourself is the most personal custom-made item possible—it's done of you, for you, by an artist of your choosing. In early America before the advent of photography, itinerant portrait artists painted their way around the country; since it could be a long time before another artist came that way again, they were often hired regardless of their talent. Today the client can select a portraitist from many outstanding artists with national reputations, choosing the one whose style is personally appealing. A good way to contact potential artists is through an art gallery. If you would like the artist to be someone relatively close to your home, visit local galleries and discuss your

needs with the staff there. Some well-known galleries, such as Portraits, Inc. in New York City, specialize in representing portrait artists nationwide. In addition, the portrait artists themselves sometimes advertise in art and home magazines. In any case, the artist or gallery should be able to provide references and photos of previous portraits.

Once the artist has been chosen, it's time for serious discussion. Some important questions need to be resolved, such as: Is the portrait to be formal or informal? How big will it be? Where will it hang? How much time will the artist need? What is the fee schedule? Answering these questions at the outset will help avoid

confusion and disappointment.

Most painted portraits are done in oils, although some artists use other mediums such as acrylics, watercolors, or pastels. Generally the artist prefers to meet face-to-face with the client for a few hours at least once. During that time the artist will get a sense of your personality and the sort of portrait you want. He or she will also make preliminary sketches and take a number of photographs. After that the artist usually returns to the studio and gets to work, delivering the finished portrait weeks or months later.

BRONZE PORTRAITS

An interesting, if more monumental, alternative to the painted por-

trait is a bronze sculpture. A bronze portrait is usually a head-and-shoulders bust, although anything from just the head to an oversized full-length portrait can be created. The process of selecting the artist is much the same as for paintings, and the artist will proceed at first in the same way. The sculpture itself is created from clay on an armature; it is later cast in bronze at a foundry under the artist's supervision.

PHOTOGRAPHS

An evocative photographic portrait is usually considerably less expensive than a fine-art portrait. It has the additional advantages of taking far less time and of being reproducible. There are many excellent local photographers who can take a good portrait photograph in a studio setting. To select a photographer in your area, visit the studio and ask to see his or her portrait portfolio. Generally, the arrangement you make with the photographer will include several poses and a specified number of prints in different sizes. The photographer almost always retains the negatives. On a nationwide basis, the famed Yousuf Karsh visits various cities on a regular basis; Bachrach has studios in a number of cities and visits others. Joshua Hendon, one of the best-known childrens' photographers, has a studio in New York City and frequently arranges sittings in other cities.

91

GOLF CLUBS

Every golf club from Kenneth Smith is handmade to fit the client's personal specifications, and then stamped with a registration number, left.

"Golf," Sir Winston Churchill once said, "is a game devised by the Devil with instruments ill-suited to the purpose." No golfer would argue with the first part of that statement, but those with custom-fitted clubs might disagree with the second.

In the art and science of selecting golf clubs, one must take into account all these factors: the head design, the shaft flex, the club lie, the club length, and the swing weight.

Perimeter-weighted head designs, pioneered by Ping, are the most popular head designs among golfers today. Thin in the center, these "forgiving" irons and woods have extra weight in the heel and toe of the head.

The shaft of the club has an important effect on distance and accuracy. Stiff shafts will help you hit the ball straighter; the stronger you are, the stiffer the shaft should be. The finest modern shafts are made of graphite, which on aver-

age is an ounce lighter than the lightest steel shafts of earlier days. Particularly for older players or those with a light swing, graphite shafts, which are lighter and more flexible than metal ones, can be a big help.

The lie of the club (the angle between the shaft and the ground when the sole of the club is flat on the ground) is another important consideration, and one where custom fitting is very helpful for senior players and those who are taller or shorter than average. The lie on a custom golf club can be varied as much as ten degrees from the norm.

The longer the club shaft, the greater the speed and thus the greater the distance the ball can be hit. Distance without accuracy is no help, however. Custom-fitted clubs provide exactly the right length for the individual player.

Finally, swing weight must be considered. Although this is an oft-discussed topic among golf-

ers, there is much confusion and little universal agreement about its importance. Generally swing weight refers to the ratio between the weight of the head and the total weight of the golf club. Most golfers prefer heavy clubs for accuracy and light clubs for distance, but the weight of the club is affected not only by the head but also by the shaft and the grip. Ultimately the decision on the best swing weight is a personal and aesthetic one, based on the look and feel of the club.

CUSTOM CLUB MAKERS

Most of the highly regarded golf club manufacturers, such as Ping, offer custom fitting of standard clubs through golf shop pros. Minor adjustments of the shaft length and grip for individual needs can be made.

The custom clubs can be ordered directly from the maker or through a professional at a golf

shop. The world's largest custom club maker is Kenneth Smith Golf Clubs of Kansas City, Missouri. These handsome clubs are handmade to fit the individual player's physical size, playing style, and natural swing. Each club is stamped with the owner's initials and a registration number. Kenneth Smith clubs are so finely made that many remain in use after fifty years of regular play. All club heads are forged; custom grips and a range of thirty-six shaft flexes are among the many choices offered. Kenneth Smith produces custom-made clubs designed particularly for women and left-handed players, and also offers special clubs such as drivers with larger heads for very strong hitters.

Ted Sheftic Custom Clubs of New Oxford, Pennsylvania, has been crafting golf clubs since 1969. Founder Ted Sheftic is a Class A PGA golf pro, and is regarded as one of golf's most successful teachers. His unusual but very successful driver, the "Hooky," is designed to help the many golfers who hook their shots solve the problem.

Custom clubs from ProGroup, Inc. of Ooltewah, Tennessee, are made by the same craftsmen who have been making Arnold Palmer's golf clubs for nearly three decades.

This lightweight, eight-foot Battenkill trout rod from Orvis, below, is ornamented with a bird's-eye maple reel seat and nickel silver hardware.

The Limited Editions series rods from Thomas & Thomas, opposite page, are specially constructed rods produced each year in limited numbers. Proud possessors of these rods include the Prince and Princess of Wales.

The fine art of fly fishing was developed on the fast-flowing chalk streams of England. American anglers soon realized that the trout streams of New York's Adirondack Mountains posed many of the same challenges, and American fly-fishing was born. Silently stalking and then presenting a fly to a wary trout remains one of angling's greatest challenges. The right rod, properly balanced and of the correct length, won't guarantee a catch, but it will certainly make the fishing more fun.

Choosing the right fly rod is partly a matter of science and partly a matter of aesthetics. Two factors that must be considered together are the weight of the line you are most likely to use (this will affect the size of the flies) and where you usually fish. If most of your fishing is on narrow trout streams under 50 feet in width, you will probably use a lighter line size of anywhere from one to six, and thus need a rod anywhere from 7 to 8½ feet long. If you fish for trout on wide rivers or in lakes, a heavier line and a rod from 8½ to

9 feet long are called for. Those who fish for bass, salmon, steelhead, bonefish, or tarpon need correspondingly heavier lines and longer rods; some salmon rods are 15 feet long.

The next consideration is the rod material. The choices are graphite, boron/graphite, fiberglass and bamboo. Bamboo is the overwhelming first choice for the finest custom-made rods, followed by graphite. In the end, after considering other factors, such as the taper of the rod, the final decision is often made on the basis of sheer beauty; a finely

made fly rod is a work of art. Exquisitely sensitive and graceful custom-made fly rods are the result of careful selection of materials combined with careful craftsmanship. The best bamboo rods are made from tonkin cane, also known as tea-stick bamboo. The rodmaker seeks only those rare canes with rich, uniform color; hand rubbing to bring out the natural polish is the only finish. Perfect tapers, reel seats of exotic woods, cork grips designed to fit the hand perfectly, and guides held on with meticulous thread windings are the hallmarks.

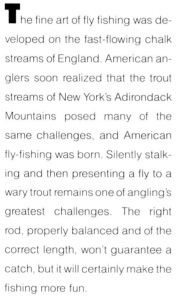

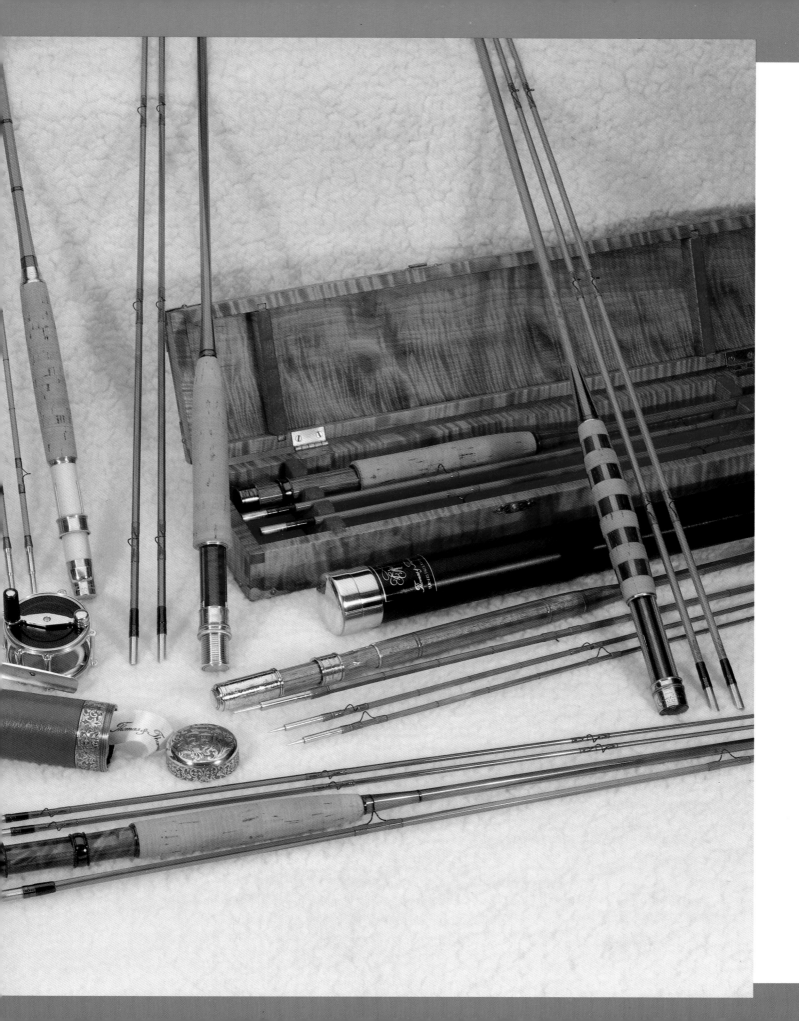

Powell Rod company makes fine graphite fly rods, below.

98

THE MAKERS

Fine rods made from bamboo or graphite are available from several sources. One of the best-known is Orvis, which also claims to be America's oldest mail order company. Bamboo Battenkill rods from Orvis are beautifully made, with elegant bird's-eye maple reel seats and nickel silver hardware. Each rod is individually registered and can be personalized with your name. A newer company, which has established an enviable reputation for excellence since its founding in 1969, is Thomas & Thomas. Each of the few Individualist R rods from Thomas & Thomas requires more than forty-five hours of skilled handwork to complete. Each rod carries an individual serial numbers, and can be personalized with your initials on the butt or custom engraved on the rod fittings. Also available every year from Thomas & Thomas are Heritage R limited-edition rods. These collector's items now sell for much more than their original high price.

The Powell Rod Company, now involving the fourth generation of Powells, makes graphite rods that rival the finest bamboo. The options on these made-to-order rods are unlimited down to the last and finest detail.

The ultimate in custom fly rods comes not only at a high price but with a long wait. To get a handmade rod by such famed individual craftsmen as Hoagie Carmichael, Jr., Per Brandon, or Walter Carpenter can take months. However, dedicated fly fishers are a patient lot, and for them the wait for the perfect rod is well worthwhile.

Three outstanding reels are crafted in a special hundred-edition set for specific types of fishing: baitcasting, spinning, and spincasting, below.

BICYCLES

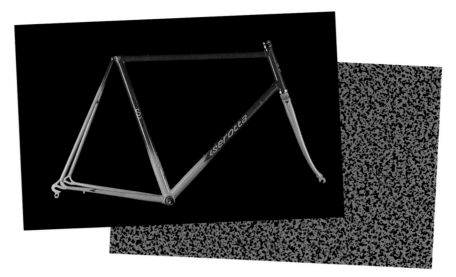

The Colorado bicy-
cle frame, built by
Ben Serotta, left,
incorporates over-
size tubes. This de-
sign is used by the
highly successful
7-Eleven bicycle
racing team.

As more and more people are discovering, bicycling is one of the best and most enjoyable forms of exercise. Runners are prone to injuries and swimmers get to look at the bottom of the pool; bike riders get a safe, convenient workout and enjoy the scenery as well.

Most bike riders are content with a high-quality, mass-manufactured bicycle with good standard equipment. However, those who get serious about their biking, or those with special needs, find that custom-made bicycles are the only way to ride.

The core of any bicycle, whether it is a standard ten-speed road bike, an ATB (all-terrain bicycle, also called a mountain bike), or a professional racing bike, is the frame. On custom bicycles, the frame is hand-constructed to exact specifications. The primary factors considered include the biker's body dimensions (height, weight, torso length, and so on) and the intended use of the bike. Generally speaking, the tires,

brakes, derailleurs, and other features on the bike are selected from the many fine options offered by well-known manufacturers. The actual construction of a custom bike can take days if not weeks.

THE BUILDERS

There are excellent custom bike builders around the country. In California, Dave Moulton, one of the world's best-known builders, makes his Fuso Lux road bikes. Produced by hand in limited numbers, these steel-framed bikes are among the finest made. The dean of American bike-builders, Moulton started making frames in England in 1957, training with a craftsman who had been building frames since 1909. He emigrated to the United States in 1979 and set up his own shop in 1982.

Other California builders of custom bikes include Tesch Bicycle Company. The Tesch S-22 bike, built by designer Dave Tesch, is precisely handcrafted for both speed and beauty. It is

available in nine sizes and six standard colors; custom paint jobs are among the options. Exceptional mountain bikes are built by two California companies: Cunningham Applied Technology and Mountain Goat Cycles. Charlie Cunningham builds alumi-

num mountain bikes that are light, strong, and durable. Something of a purist, Cunningham does not paint his bikes, feeling that polished aluminum does not need paint to protect it, and that a fancy paint job would only be obliterated by the hard off-road use for which his bikes are made. ATB bikes from Mountain Goat Cycles offer crisp handling and all-day comfort along with powerful performance. Mountain Goat takes the opposite approach from Cunningham and is famous for unique paint finishes and designs.

For those who like togetherness, hand-built tandem bicycles made by Santana Cycles are available in racing, sport, and all-terrain models.

Great custom bikes are not confined to California. One of the most famous of all custom bike builders is Benjamin Serotta of Middle Grove, New York. Serotta uses steel to make his racing,

Serious bicycles designed for a woman's body, left, are crafted by engineer Georgena Terry of Terry Precision Bicycles. The radical but effective design uses a smaller front wheel.

101

ATB, and road bikes. These are not ordinary bicycles—several members of the 1984 and 1988 Olympic team raced on Serotta bicycles, as do members of the 7-Eleven racing team. In Connecticut Peter Weigle builds a limited number of clean, elegant frames by hand; in Pennsylvania Tom Kellog of Spectrum Cycles builds individually tailored bicycles that have been used by Olympians and professional racers.

An obvious fact that is only just beginning to be noted by major bicycle manufacturers is that women have different bodies than men, and thus require different bicycles. Custom bike makers, of course, have known this for a long time. Foremost among them is Georgena Terry. Trained as a mechanical engineer, Terry realized that women have shorter torsos than men. She struck upon the radical idea of building a modified frame having a shorter top tube (allowing the rider to reach the handlebars without stretching). For short women, Terry offers a

Mountain bikes from Cunningham Applied Technology, above, are built to be both sturdy and light— important for bicycles used over rough trails.

bike with a front wheel that is smaller than the back wheel. This allows better steering and leg clearance, making the bike comfortable, safe, and easy to ride.

Taking AIR-SOLE® technology a step further, Nike offers the Air Pressure basketball shoe, below, inflatable for a customized fit and maximum performance.

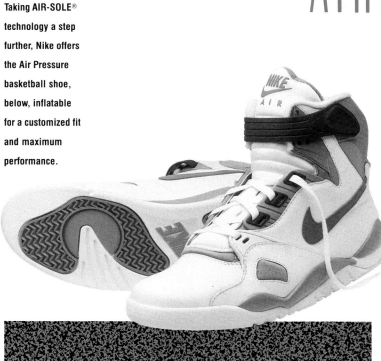

The serious athlete's ongoing quest for perfection is reflected in the design of modern athletic shoes. Conceptual breakthroughs combine with new materials to create shoes that enhance both comfort and performance.

RUNNING SHOES

All feet are different, even on the same person. To help provide an exact fit, Reebok has introduced the Pump running shoe. Complete with built-in air compressor, the Pump can be inflated around the ankle collar and at the front of the foot to provide a customized fit.

True custom running shoes have been made by Bart Hersey of the Hersey Custom Shoe Company in Farmington, Maine, since 1982. These outstanding shoes are an excellent value for any runner, whether serious or casual, but they are particularly helpful for

those with unusual needs. Every Hersey shoe has a handmade double reverse flare construction at the heel to add strength, width, and stability and to reduce the effects of pronation and supination. (Pronation, or turning the foot inward, and supination, or turning the foot outward, are major causes of the injuries that plague runners.) The Hersey shoe is also an excellent choice for women runners, whose needs are not well served by most mass-produced shoes. Women's feet strike the ground at a different angle than men's, and their heels tend to be much narrower in proportion to the front of their feet. Hersey's shoes for women accommodate these differences with shoes that are functional and very durable. For both men and women, Hersey easily handles such common requests as different size shoes for

each foot, special toe boxes, extra sole protection, Achilles notches in the heel counter, size adjustments for orthotic inserts, and completely nonleather shoes for those who object to animal materials. Any and all other special requests are welcome.

OTHER SHOES

The ideal pair of basketball shoes has good cushioning to protect against impact shock, is supportive to stabilize the foot during lateral moves and jump landings, and is generally responsive and maneuverable. The Nike Air Pressure basketball shoe combines the firm's revolutionary Air-Sole® technology in the sole with a new Air-Fit collar at the ankle for superior performance. The Air-Fit collar consists of air units inside the ankle collar that are inflated with a hand pump to provide a customized fit. Reebok also makes inflatable basketball shoes.

Hiking shoes need to be both durable and comfortable, qualities for which custom boots from Peter Limmer and Sons of Intervale, New Hampshire, have been famous for three generations. Made from traditional leather in regular front-lace or Tyrolean side-lace styles, these hard-wearing hiking shoes are worn by mountaineers on expeditions all over the world.

103

ATHLETIC EQUIPMENT

In every culture at every period in history, weapons have been embellished with high artistic skill. Ever since their invention in the fifteenth century, firearms have attracted the talents of artists who work in metal and wood. The wooden stock of a rifle, often made from fine walnut, and the handle of a pistol, usually made of wood, ivory, or metal, can be intricately carved and inlaid; the metal of the rest of the firearm can be beautifully engraved. Many custom-made rifles, shotguns, and even some pistols are designed to be functional hunting weapons of the very best quality. Often, however, a custom-engraved firearm is a work of art made solely for the collector. These weapons can be fired, but they rarely are, because firing can sharply reduce their value.

Major firearms manufacturers such as Colt, Remington, and U.S. Repeating Arms Company (makers of Winchester guns) have custom shops that will engrave the firearm to the customer's specifications and produce commemorative engravings. Smaller manufacturers such as Freedom Arms, Champlin Rifles, Weatherby, and Kimber offer handcrafted and limited-production guns with more extensive customizing, including special stocks and elaborate engraving.

The finest gun engraving is fine art in miniature form. By universal acclaim, the best gun engraver in America today is Winston G. Churchill of Proctorsville, Vermont. Fantastically detailed and accurate, Churchill's work is avidly collected by individuals and museums, including the Smithsonian Institution. He adorns the sideplates, trigger guards, floorplates, grip caps, and other parts of the guns with hunting scenes of breathtaking realism. Churchill is a master of the engraver's arsenal: he uses sculpted and flat relief, stippling, inlaying, engraving, and scrollwork in a number of styles. In addition to engraving guns, Churchill also creates mahogany presentation cases handsomely detailed in brass and complete with engraved and gold-plated accessories.

True custom gunsmithing from start to finish is a demanding and time-consuming art. Custom guns from such famed makers as Griffin & Howe in New York, or James Purdey or Holland & Holland in London, can take many months if not years (as many as ten from Purdey) to be delivered, at prices that can be truly breathtaking. These firms also offer special engraving, special stocks, commemorative and limited-edition guns, and beautifully cased presentation revolvers.

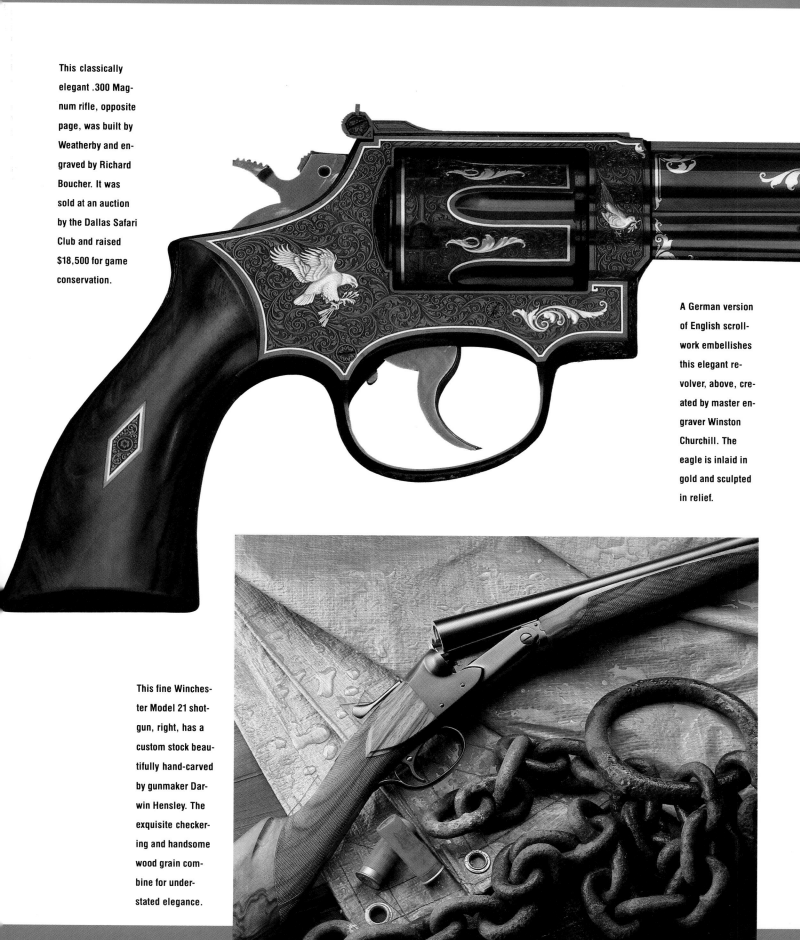

This classically elegant .300 Magnum rifle, opposite page, was built by Weatherby and engraved by Richard Boucher. It was sold at an auction by the Dallas Safari Club and raised $18,500 for game conservation.

A German version of English scrollwork embellishes this elegant revolver, above, created by master engraver Winston Churchill. The eagle is inlaid in gold and sculpted in relief.

This fine Winchester Model 21 shotgun, right, has a custom stock beautifully hand-carved by gunmaker Darwin Hensley. The exquisite checkering and handsome wood grain combine for understated elegance.

CHAPTER 6
VEHICLES

The Bentley Turbo R, left, combines effortless power and tight handling with extraordinary refinement, quietness, and comfort. It is powered by a turbo-charged intercooled 6.75 liter V-8 engine. (Reprinted by permission of Rolls-Royce Motor Cars Inc.)

Building a Rolls-Royce today is a slow, painstaking process. Current models take between three and six months to build. The assembly line moves just a few feet each day, and only after the craftsmen involved are satisfied that their work is as nearly perfect as human ingenuity can make it. The amount of hand labor in every Rolls-Royce is incredible. Only ten men in the world can make the signature Rolls-Royce radiator grille, which is crafted entirely by hand. Each grille bears the famous interlinked Rolls-Royce emblem, and, unobtrusively at the back, a second set of initials—the signature of the individual craftsman who made it. Every engine is hand-assembled, with one craftsman taking final responsibility for each one. The famed Flying Lady hood-ornament mascot, known more formally as *The Spirit of Ec-*

stasy, was commissioned from sculptor Charles Sykes in 1911. To this day, every mascot is cast using the lost-wax technique and finished by hand, making every Flying Lady slightly different. Quality of the highest order prevails in the interior of the car as well. Only the finest leather is used for the upholstery, the carpeting is of the finest lamb's wool, and veneers used on the instrument panel come from specially selected Italian and California walnut. The goal is perfection, and it is achieved as nearly as is humanly possible.

Among the current Rolls-Royce models is the Corniche II, a classic convertible considered by many to be the most glamorous car ever built by the company. The Silver Spur, and the somewhat smaller Silver Spirit, are formal sedans; both are successful mar-

riages of luxury, comfort, and practicality.

Four Bentley models are designed and engineered by Rolls-Royce craftsmen. All offer speed, superb road handling, and interior luxury. The flagship of the Bentley range is the Turbo R, introduced in the autumn of 1988. The most powerful Bentley ever built, this five passenger sedan cruises comfortably at 135 mph and goes from zero to sixty in 6.7 seconds. Bentley racing cars dominated the European racing circuits in the 1920s; the Turbo R combines Bentley performance with the comfort and quality traditionally supplied by Rolls-Royce craftsmen. The other Bentleys are not far behind: the classically styled Mulsanne S sedan; the Bentley Eight; and the Continental touring car, with classic, sweeping lines and superb comfort.

OTHER CAR BUILDERS

Every Aston Martin Lagonda motorcar is hand-built for its owner, and customized to the point that the chassis carries the owner's initials. The amount of labor that goes into these cars is little short of astonishing. The sleek Aston Martin Vantage Volante high-performance convertible is the end result of over four months of individual hand-building at the factory in Buckinghamshire, England.

Cars from Lotus in Hethel, England, are world-famous for their handling, performance, and style, in equal proportions. The Esprit, for example, provides a remarkably supple ride, goes from zero to sixty in just 5.2 seconds, and is meticulously finished, down to a hand-stitched leather steering wheel. More than 500 man-hours go into the making of every Esprit.

The world's fastest four-seater convertible is the Vantage Volante, above, from Aston Martin Lagonda Ltd. It accelerates from zero to sixty mph in just 5.2 seconds.

With a top speed of over 155 mph, and a beautifully smooth ride, the turbocharged Lotus Esprit, below, is one of the world's most desirable sports cars.

111

The Porsche 928 S4, left, features world-class performance and a lengthy list of standard appointments, including an on-board computer and an electric sliding sunroof. From first to last, every Morgan, below, at the factory has the owner's name printed on the paperwork. The craftspeople—who build them by hand—sign each piece with their personal identification numbers.

The first and most enduring of the true sports cars is the Morgan. Made in Worcestershire, England, every Morgan has the name of its future owner on it from the moment construction begins—these cars are custom-made in the fullest sense of the word. The roadster design of a modern Morgan, with its canvas top, mud guards, and low-cut doors, is little changed from 1936. Morgans are still hand-crafted on a wooden (not steel) frame, and only about 500 are made in a year.

Lamborghini, the world-renowned Italian specialty car maker, was acquired by the Chrysler Corporation in 1987. The company continues to produce its famous high-performance sports cars, particularly the famed Countach. This sharply styled mid-engine car, with its signature gull-wing doors and astonishing performance (zero to sixty in 4.7 seconds) recently celebrated its twenty-fifth year with an anniversary edition limited to 400 vehicles. Lamborghini also produces

the LM002, the ultimate four-wheel-drive utility vehicle. Just over 16 feet long, 6 feet high, and 6 feet 8 inches wide, the luxurious LM002 is powered by an engine derived from the Countach powerplant.

A newcomer to the luxury auto market is the Bitter Type 3. This convertible roadster combines German engineering with Italian craftsmanship to create a car of understated elegance. The interior of the Type 3 features, among other details, hand-stitched Italian glove, leather upholstery, African rosewood trim, and a gold production-number plate displayed on the console.

Porsche cars have long been among the finest examples of the successful integration of luxury and very high performance. Outstanding performance, superb ergonomics, and a lengthy list of standard appointments make the flagship Porsche 928 S4 one of the finest Porsches ever made.

Advanced European styling combines with spirited American performance in the ASC/McLaren Limited-edition sports convertible. Among the available custom features on this vehicle are the console, all-leather interior, and exterior paint and accents. ASC markets the car through selected Ford dealers; each convertible is backed by both Ford and ASC warranty service programs.

Lamborghini, the world-renowned Italian specialty car maker, marked its twenty-fifth year with this limited edition of the famous mid-engined Countach, above.

The custom exterior paint and accents and custom leather interior of the ASC/McLaren limited-edition sports convertible, below, are just some of the standard features.

CAR CUSTOMIZING AND ACCESSORIES

Custom installations of state-of-the-art speakers, left, and other electronic accessories are a specialty at Creative Car Stereo. Speakers color-matched to the car's interior (for aesthetic and security reasons) are another specialty. Custom-built exotic automobiles from Koenig Specials of Munich, opposite page, are available through Imaage Worldwide. Every car is manufactured under strict Bavarian quality standards to the individual requirements of the owner.

114

It is possible to make a fine automobile even better by adding custom components not available through the factory. The process is probably best illustrated by the AMG Company, based in Germany. AMG starts with the superb Mercedes-Benz motorcars that roll off the production line in Stuttgart and takes them one step further. The added enhancements are designed to expand the car's already significant capabilities to perform at the highest levels of driving. To that end, extensive modifications to the car's aerodynamics, wheels and tires, suspension, power train, powerplant, interior, and other styling details can be made exactly to the most demanding client's specifications.

The classic American Corvette sports car, made by General Motors, is a favorite for customizing. SCM Motors converts Corvettes into Culébras, exotic cars with classic Italian styling. The conversion process consists of building an entirely new body onto the Corvette's inner structure (this leaves the factory warranty intact). Each SCM conversion is handcrafted with special attention to detail. In addition to adding such luxurious interior features as custom-made burled walnut dash, center console, and door panels, and custom Hayashi racing wheels, SCM can customize the power train, the suspension, and the brakes. The large amount of skilled hand work required to build a Culébra takes six to ten weeks to complete.

One of the premier builders of custom Corvettes is Graddy Richards of Distinctly Styled Corvettes, better known as DSC among aficionados. DSC offers in-dividualized customizing with a broadly diverse array of options and accessories. As the ultimate personal service, DSC staff members are frequently flown to construct the car on the client's premises. DSC has expanded its offerings to include custom conversion for almost any domestic or foreign car or truck in addition to Corvettes.

Limited-edition, numbered Corvette coupes and convertibles are made by Greenwood Automotive Performance. Aerodynamic styling, suspension modifications, extraordinary interiors, and extra soundproofing make these cars extremely comfortable. Hand-rubbed paintwork gives the cars a gleaming, mirrorlike finish, and numerous exterior and interior accessories, such as targa roll bars and mobile sound systems, can be added.

Even an ordinary car can be customized with special electronics (car stereos and alarm systems are the most common), interior accessories, special wheels, mascots, and a personalized car cover to protect it all.

ELECTRONICS

Roaring down the open road while listening to a great car stereo playing your favorite music is one of life's more enjoyable experiences. But why stop at just a fine stereo? The engineers and craftsmen at Ultrasmith Systems can install an amazing array of sophisticated electronic equipment. In addition to custom-made speaker enclosures and color television, your car can have an alarm system, a mobile fax machine and cellular phone, a remote radar detector, an exotic skin interior, a concealed safe, and other toys for grown-ups—even an automatic toll booth window.

WHEELS

Master engraver Art Cordiero of Status Wheels offers personalized, gold-plated, hand-engraved wheels for fine automobiles. Done in the traditional manner with hammer and chisel, the engraving is applied to the wire spokes and wheels, then electroplated with 24-karat gold with a silver or chrome overlay for a unique, two-tone effect. The wheels are available for such fine automobiles as Lamborghini, Mercedes-Benz, Ferrari, Rolls-Royce, Porsche, BMW, Cadillac, Jaguar, and other exotic cars. Custom engraving is also available for bumpers and interiors.

CAR MASCOTS

An imported, unusual car mascot from Mascots Unlimited is a great way to add an individual touch to your car. The British royal family has long admired mascots from this company. The Queen's Land Rover sports a silver labrador retriever, while Prince Charles has a polo player on his Granada. For commoners, a wide range of horses, cows, bulls, dogs, birds, fish, and other creatures is available. All are hand-finished in chrome plate or enamel for outstanding resistance to corrosion. Custom enameling and mascots made of silver or gold can be ordered. Particularly popular subjects for custom enameling are race horses with jockeys wearing the owner's own racing silks.

CAR COVERS

After spending a small fortune on customizing your car, it makes sense to protect your investment from damaging sunlight, dust, pollutants, and tree droppings with a custom car cover. The largest manufacturer of specialized car protection products in the world is Covercraft. With over 17,000 patterns and four different fabrics to choose from, Covercraft can provide a perfect fit for any vehicle. Covercraft also makes custom car masks (also known as nose bras) to protect the front end

of cars against nicks, scratches, stones, bugs, and other damaging road debris.

Custom cars covers from Beverly Hills Motoring Accessories are available only in heavy cotton in the company's trademarked blue color. The covers can be custom embroidered with logos, license numbers, names, initials, or special messages. Beverly Hills Motoring Accessories offers a wide range of car-customizing products, including car masks, wheels, seats, steering wheels, wood accessories, and more.

EXECUTIVE ARMORING CORPORATION

EAC manufactures armored vehicles in a broad range of configurations and levels of perfection. Virtually any automobile can be protected with inconspicuous, lightweight armor and still maintain its original appearance and driving characteristics. In addition to "invisibly" armoring a vehicle, EAC can provide options such as tear gas, smoke screen, and oil slick dispensers; gun ports; and a combined remote start and bomb scan feature.

LIMOUSINES

The best way to arrive in style is to arrive in a luxurious, custom-built limousine, equipped with everything—including a color television, advanced stereo sound system and, for those who feel the need, armor plating.

A custom limousine begins with the purchase of a standard luxury automobile, often a Ca-dillac, Lincoln, Mercedes-Benz, or other large sedan. The vehicle is shipped to the limousine maker for the work of conversion. Work-men systematically strip the brand-new, very expensive vehi-cle of its luxurious interior, reduc-ing the car to a hollow shell. Then, using blowtorches, they literally cut the vehicle in half. The exten-sions that lengthen the body (usu-ally adding between 48 and 60 inches) and add extra headroom are welded into place, and the basic systems of the car are re-built. One reason limousines have such a smooth, quiet ride is the extra soundproofing, which is ap-plied during the rebuilding pro-cess. Numerous safety features for extra reliability are also added at this point.

While all this is going on, craftsmen are at work creating the interior elements. What those will be is up to customer, but there's very little that *can't* be done. It could be a 17-foot vehicle with an interior that is a rolling office, com-plete with fax machine and paper

The large pas-senger area of Wide-Body lim-ousines from Cor-porate Coach-works, above, make them among the most spacious available.

shredder. Or it could be the world's longest limousine, built by Ultra Limousine Company: 102 feet, with seating for 25, and such convenient extra touches as a mi-crowave oven and an aquarium.

Until fairly recently, most lim-ousine sales were to demanding personal buyers. Today, the livery market accounts for the bulk of

118

limousine sales, but personal buyers can still expect red-carpet treatment from the premier limousine builders. All limousines are crafted to order at the builder's shop, but the purchase is generally arranged through the builder's authorized regional dealers.

ALLEN COACHWORKS
Today one of the leading personal limousine manufacturers is Carlos Allen of Allen Coachworks. Sixty or so luxury features are standard (mahogany window sills with veneer inlays, quadraphonic speaker system and designer tissue dispenser, to name a few) on the average Allen limousine. For those who want the luxury of a limousine but prefer to keep a lower profile, Allen makes the very handsome Lusso executive sedan, built on a Cadillac Brougham body with a 26-inch wheelbase extension.

Mercedes-Benz limousines from Allen Coachworks, above, are always custom made to the client's specifications. Frequently requested amenities include door-mounted desks and mahogany window sills.

119

RECREATIONAL VEHICLES

Recreational vehicles with self-contained living quarters come in a bewildering variety of shapes and sizes. The only RVs that can truly be said to be custom-built, however, are the top-of-the-line class A motor homes. These bus-sized vehicles let their owners travel the country equipped with all the comforts and luxuries of home. In fact, since the average motor home is well over 30 feet long and some 8 feet wide, the interior space is often larger than a typical one-bedroom city apartment. The cost can be larger as well—a typical motor home RV costs well into six figures.

Customizing an RV offers many of the same satisfactions and rewards as building a house. The builders take pride in their ability to accommodate any request. As a result, the finest motor homes are beautiful examples of engineering and construction in-genuity. A great deal of skilled hand labor is needed to create a motor home that is rugged, safe, and also attractive. Some manufacturers, such as Marathon, begin with a commercial bus and convert it into a motor home; some, such as Airstream, start with a commercial chassis and build the rest; and others, such as Foretravel, build everything, including the chassis.

Even before any custom options are added, no two motor homes are ever alike because all the standard features—and there are many—are offered in many choices, including cabinetry, carpets, upholstery, window treatments, and colors. The array of options is startling. Telephones, stereo systems, CB radios, televisions, and VCRs, to say nothing of other advanced electronics such as rear-view TV cameras, are often added. Washers and dryers,

Motor homes from Airstream, above, feature signature aluminum fuselages. The roomy interior of a Country Coach motor home, opposite page, has plenty of space for lounging, eating, and sleeping.

instant hot-water taps, microwave ovens, water softeners, ice makers, wet bars, and other amenities are all options in the kitchen area. For extra comfort while driving, the standard pilot and co-pilot seats can be replaced with six-way power seats. The frame of the motor home itself can be modified with extra doors, observation decks, fold-out satellite dishes, awnings, exterior lighting, and panoramic windows. Of course, company artists are always on hand at the plant to create custom exterior paint schemes, graphics, and murals.

In idle moments, many a boat lover daydreams of sailing off on a round-the-world cruise to sunny harbors, leaving all troubles behind. Integral to the daydream, of course, is a magnificent yacht, bigger and better than whatever craft the boat lover currently owns. Fortunately, some dreams can come true, and a custom-built boat is one of them.

A truly custom-built yacht, designed by a naval architect from the keel up specifically for the purchaser, can take months or even years to build, and can cost an amazing amount. In some cases the designer will also build the boat, but often the buyer selects a boatyard to do the actual construction. Much more common than true custom boats are basic designs (called production boats) that are then built and customized, inside and out—often extensively—by the boatyard to the buyer's taste. Generally, customizing is done to modify the hardware and electronics, select the paint

scheme, and design the cabin interiors, although further customizing is often added.

The decision to design and build a customized boat is not one to be taken lightly. It requires a large commitment of the purchaser's time, patience, and interest as well as money. The reward is getting a vessel that is unique.

DESIGNERS AND BUILDERS

Some of the world's finest production yachts are Swans built by Nautor in Finland. Since their introduction in the 1960s, Swan boats, ranging in size from 36 to 86 feet, have gained a worldwide reputation for speed, elegance, and comfort. Nautor takes pride in offering great flexibility when customizing a yacht to the purchaser's requirements.

Yachts from John G. Alden, Inc. have combined integrity with elegance, safety, and speed since 1909. Alden has produced many superior production de-

This 18-foot lifeboat tender, above, left, was hand-built in wood by the Cannell Boatbuilding Company; the designer is well-known L. Francis Herreshoff. Fast and comfortable cruising pleasure is the goal of Nautour's Swan, as shown by this Swan 51 yacht, above, right. *Magic Lady*, opposite page, is a 105-foot centerboard cutter designed by the naval architects at John G. Alden, Inc.

signs over the years, but the firm is probably best known today for designing very large yachts that are then built at the finest yards around the world.

Naval architect Charles W. Wittholz is a versatile designer, one who can handle both sail and power boats. His designs range from classic catboats to 90-foot sailing yachts to elegant motor yachts to reproductions such as the Revolutionary sloop-of-war *Providence*, now sailing for the Seaport '76 Foundation of Newport, Rhode Island.

Henry R. Hinckley founded the

Hinckley Company in 1928; by the 1940s, the firm had grown to become the largest producer of wooden sailboats with inboard auxiliary engines in the United States. The introduction of fiberglass construction in the 1950s ushered in a new age of mass production in the boating industry—but not at Hinckley. Today, the Hinckley Company remains one of the best boat builders in America, but produces only sixteen to eighteen fiberglass sailboats a year. Hinckley boats range in size from 40 to 60 feet. A crew of seventy-five master craftsmen build the boats, which can take anywhere from six months to a year to complete and require between 8,000 and 20,000 man-hours apiece. (By way of contrast, a Mercedes-Benz automobile takes about 125 man-hours to make.)

A proper sailing yacht must be a harmonious blend of technical sophistication, mechanical integrity, and artistic beauty. Sailing boats from Pacific Seacraft meet all these requirements. Pacific Seacraft makes small, beautiful boats for the cruising sailor. The firm's largest boat is forty-three feet long. All the others are smaller, but in yachts size is far from all. Every Pacific Seacraft boat is built with the individual owner's involvement, from the choice of hardware to the outstanding woodwork to the interior design of the cabin. This sort of craftsmanship takes time, however—Pacific Seacraft builds only about 120 boats a year.

The craftsmen at Cannell Boatbuilding designed and built this 18-foot pulling boat, above. As can be seen here, no effort has been spared in making this lightweight boat.

With hundreds of custom yacht designs to their credit, the firm of Hartog & Rosenbaum, Inc. can provide innovative, beautiful luxury yachts, both power and sail. Hartog & Rosenbaum work big—yachts that are over 200 feet long are well within the firm's experience, as are "armored" yachts featuring fortified control rooms, underwater surveillance, secure

The Classique, right, from Xylem is a 32-foot performance powerboat. The structure is made from a lightweight but very strong laminated veneer; it combines the beauty of wood with easy maintenance.

telecommunications, and even on-board defense systems. Recently Hartog & Rosenbaum have branched out into custom floating islands. Fantasies come true, the "islands" are some 2,000 square feet in size and contain structures complete with staterooms, kitchens, wine cellars, and a fireplace. The islands also have beaches, landscaping, boat slips, and more. They are completely self-contained and can be moved anywhere there's water.

The Xylem Classique, above, is powered by twin 420-horsepower Mercury engines; two fuel tanks each hold 100 gallons.

There was once a time when a journey by train meant elegance, romance, and occasionally intrigue. The very names of the grand trains—The Orient Express, the Empire Builder, the Broadway Limited—are reminiscent of a magical era. For those who love train travel, the pleasure of a luxuriously appointed private rail car is not entirely a thing of the past. Many of the private rail cars once owned by the wealthy were scrapped by the 1950s, but almost as many survived, to be purchased and lovingly restored by enthusiasts.

Northern Rail Car Corporation is a leader in rail car repair and refurbishment. In addition to the extensive mechanical and electric work required to bring an old rail car up to modern safety standards, Northern Rail Car has an in-house cabinetry shop to restore and build custom interiors. Most owners want the old-fashioned luxury of the original rail car interior, with its mahogany and plush design, but also want the convenience of air-conditioning, contemporary bathrooms, and a modern kitchen, including such extra touches as an icemaker and dishwasher. Northern Rail Car can install or modify open-end platforms (the sort that added the words "whistle-stop tour" to the political vocabulary), and will paint the car in the owner's private colors (called livery).

Restoring a rail car is an expensive proposition, and the costs of maintaining and operating it can be very high. To use your railcar, special arrangements must be made well in advance with Amtrak. For a fairly hefty fee

The comfortable elegance of a bygone era returns in this sumptuous private observation car, opposite page and above, restored by Northern Rail Car Corporation.

the railcar is attached to a train (usually passenger) that is going where you want to go; arrangements to leave one train and connect with another can also be made. Some rail car owners offset part of the cost by chartering their cars to private individuals for unusual trips. Over a hundred private rail cars are available for chartering; for more information, contact the American Association of Private Railroad Car Owners.

127

CHOCOLATE

When Christopher Columbus returned to Spain from America for the first time, he brought with him from the New World some uninteresting dark beans—cacao beans, the source of chocolate. The court was not impressed.

When Hernan Cortez conquered the Aztecs in Mexico in 1519, he was introduced to a drink called chocolatl, made from cacao beans. The taste of the beverage was very bitter, and Cortez was not impressed.

When the Spanish conquistadors brought chocolatl back to Spain, however, various persons unknown were inspired to add sugar, cinnamon, and vanilla to the cacao, and to serve the result-

Master chef Albert Kumin is known for his fantastic desserts. His skills as a chocolatier are evident, above.

ing concoction hot. The new drink was delicious, and the aristocrats of Spain were impressed at last.

For decades the art of producing chocolate was a Spanish secret, but by the 1650s chocolate was a popular drink in France, and by 1657 it had reached England. In 1876 a revolutionary development took place: milk chocolate for eating was invented in Switzerland. Smooth and velvety fondant chocolate, ideal for con-

fectionery, was developed soon after, and the art of the chocolatier was born.

One of the best-known chocolatiers in America is Austrian-born Gunther Heiland, president of Desserts International, Inc. His dessert creations of all sorts have won him many international awards, but his most magnificent masterpieces are his chocolate sculptures.

Chocolatier Richard Donnelly creates handcrafted wine bottles of pure chocolate and fills them with roasted, chocolate-coated California almonds. The bottle arrives in an elegant gift box; other fine chocolates, made to order, are also available.

An intriguing, unusual and very personal chocolate specialty is offered by Chocolate Photos: your portrait in chocolate. Working from any photograph in printed form (black-and-white or color), Chocolate Photos creates a portrait mold that is then filled with chocolate to create an embossed image, also featuring the name of the person, on chocolate squares. Chocolate portraits ordered by mail take two to four weeks for delivery (the photo is returned separately). In addition to portraits, Chocolate Photos will custom-mold any message in chocolate, including wedding favors and corporate logos.

European trained chocolatier Richard Donnelly creates unusual chocolate wine bottles, filled with chocolate-coated almonds, and other made-to-order confections, opposite page.

The chief instructor at the International Center for Pastry Arts is chef Albert Kumin, creator of this magnificent cake commemorating Mozart, opposite page.

Centuries ago a wedding cake was something a guest brought to the nuptials, leaving it on a pile with the cakes brought by the other guests. The cakes were eaten after the ceremony to ensure the health and prosperity of the newlyweds. Gradually the custom of bringing cakes was replaced by the custom of providing an elaborately decorated wedding cake instead. That custom, of course, continues today. Beautifully decorated personalized wedding cakes—and cakes for birthdays, anniversaries and any other celebratory occasion—are produced by almost all outstanding bakeries and restaurants. For the ultimate in decorated cakes, however, several well-known bakers stand out.

Cile Bellefleur-Burbidge creates cake fantasies using a combination of royal frosting (which hardens when dry) and basic frosting (which remains soft; both are delicious). Her elaborate designs complement the colors, decor, and style of the occasion. The architectural details and sugar urns can be removed from the cake and saved under glass as a souvenir. Other creators of beautiful cakes for special events include Sylvia Weinstock, Albert Kumin, Maurice Bonté, Betty Van Norstand, Larry Rosenberg, and Rose Levy Beranbaum. Their cakes can be safely delivered to almost anywhere. For a really special occasion, the bakers will travel to the location and create the cake on the spot.

Cile Bellefleur-Burbidge made this one-layer bas mitzvah cake, top, decorated with flowers and butterflies.

An oval shape in shades of pink, this cake by Cile Bellefleur-Burbidge, above, is fit for Marie Antoinette. The amazing decoration is done in royal icing.

133

MAPLE SYRUP

Sugar maple trees, above and opposite page, are tapped in the early spring when the sap begins to run.

Mother Nature's bountiful harvest can be yours—even if you live deep in the heart of a large city. North Country Corporation offers genuine leases on sugar maple trees. Leaseholders receive a personalized lease document, frequent progress reports, and, in late April or early May, pure maple syrup made from the actual tree using traditional New England methods. In addition to sugar maple tree leases, North Country also offers leases on honey hives, lobster traps, cherry trees and apple trees, and time-sharing leases on smokehouses. In all cases, leaseholders are guaranteed a minimum amount—and more if Mother Nature is generous—of a pure, fresh country product.

134

By law, the sparkling wine called champagne can be made using only grapes harvested by hand, left, from the Champagne region of France. The chalky soil of the Champagne region, opposite page, is perfect for grapes. Pinot noir, pinot meunier, and chardonnay are the only varieties that may be used to make champagne.

Celebrations call for champagne. A truly special celebration calls for a truly special champagne—one that is rare, unusual, and delicious.

Wine has been made in the Champagne region of France for centuries. In the last decades of the seventeenth century, winemakers in the region, including the famed monk Dom Pierre Pérignon, discovered that under the right conditions their wines developed a natural effervescence. The first champagne houses to market the wine were formed around 1727 in Reims and Epernay.

Champagne starts with vines planted in the chalky soil around the three hundred villages of the Champagne region. Only three grape varieties may be used to make champagne: pinot noir, a black grape, supplies body, strength, and fullness of flavor; chardonnay, a white grape, gives lightness, elegance, and finesse; pinot meunier, another black grape, furnishes youth and freshness. The grapes are grown and harvested under strict regulations. No irrigation is permitted, and all harvesting must be done completely by hand.

Champagne is normally a blend of twenty, thirty, or even more still wines that has been caused to ferment a second time in the same bottle from which it will be served. The process begins in the autumn when the grapes are harvested and pressed. In the spring, the cellar master of each champagne house considers the still wines made from the juice and prepares his *cuvée*, or blend.

After blending, a small amount of yeast and sugar is added to each bottle. This causes a secondary fermentation in the bottle, producing the light, persistent froth and fine bubbles that are the hallmark of champagne. To achieve full maturity, balance, and nuances of flavor, champagne is aged for three to nine years. Secondary fermentation causes the formation of a sediment in the wine. To remove it, a technique called *remuage* or riddling is used. The bottles are placed in special racks with their necks tilted down slightly. Every day, for a period of several months, the bottles are gently shaken, turned and tilted a bit more, until they are upside-down and vertical and all the sediment has accumulated in the neck. The sediment is removed by the pro-

cess known as *dégorgement*. The neck of the bottle is placed in a freezing solution to form a small block of ice containing the sediment. Turning the bottle upright and removing the cellar cork causes internal pressure to eject the ice pellet, leaving behind a clear, translucent wine. The small amount of wine lost in disgorging is replaced by a *dosage*, a mixture of cane sugar and champagne. The proportion of sugar added determines whether the wine will be brut, very dry, dry, semi-sweet, or sweet.

The word champagne can legally be used *only* for sparkling wine made in the strictly delimited Champagne region. This information is clearly conveyed on the label. Look for the word champagne standing alone, not modified by a place name. The label must also say "produce of France" and give the location of the producer in the Champagne region. If the name of any other state or country appears, or if the phrase *méthode Champenoise* is used, the wine is not authentic champagne.

There are several different styles of champagne. The most common is nonvintage, made with a blend of wine from the current year's harvest and wines reserved from previous harvests. These wines are considered to be most representative of a particular champagne house's style. In an exceptional year vintage champagne is blended from the wines of only that year's harvest, although from many different vineyards and pressings; the year of the crop is shown on the label. *Blanc de blanc* champagnes are made exclusively with wines from the white chardonnay grape. Blanc de blanc wines are available in nonvintage, vintage, and prestige cuvée bottlings.

138

PRESTIGE CHAMPAGNES

Also known as prestige cuvées, prestige champagnes are the best a house knows how to make. These superior wines are blended from black and white grapes grown in the highest-rated vineyards, and are aged for up to eight or nine years. They usually carry a vintage date.

There are more than one hundred champagne producers in France, but only forty to fifty of them export their wine to the United States. Of those, only some make prestige cuvées—and only when the harvest is right, and only in limited amounts. Among them are Billecart Salmon, Bollinger, Bricout & Koch, de Castellane, Charbaut, Deutz, Gosset, Heidsieck & Cie. Monopole, Jac-

A barrel of very rare Grande Champagne cognac ages quietly, below.

quart, Jacquesson & Fils, Krug, Laurent Perrier, Möet et Chandon, Mumm, Perrier Jouet, Piper Heidsieck, Pol Roger, Pommery et Greno, Louis Roederer, Ruinart Père et Fils and Veuve Clicquot.

ROSÉ CHAMPAGNES

Deriving their color from the skins of the black grapes, and varying in tint from pale salmon to rich berry, rosé champagnes are becoming increasingly popular. These champagnes are available in nonvintage, vintage, and prestige bottlings. Because rosé champagnes are difficult to produce, not every champagne house will produce them; consequently, they are relatively rare. Indeed, rosé champagne represents only about 2 percent of total champagne production.

ENJOYING CHAMPAGNE

A wide selection of fine champagnes can be found at any good wine store. It is generally sold in standard bottles of 750 ml, but quarter bottles (splits) and half bottles can be had. For major celebrations, larger bottles are available, although the wine store may need advance notice. Magnum bottles hold 1.5 liters (two bottles); the Jereboam holds four bottles, the Methusalem holds eight, and the Salmanazar holds twelve.

The Hine aging cellars, or *paradis*, on the Quai de l'Orangerie in Jarnac, left, are filled with barrels of cognac.

COGNAC

The production of a fine and rare cognac begins with ugni blanc grapes grown in the chalky limestone soil and mild maritime climate of the Charente Valley in southwestern France. The growing area of the valley is divided into six vineyard regions, or crus. The finest crus are considered to be the Grande Champagne, Petite Champagne, Borderies, and Fins Bois, all located closest to the center of the region. Grapes are harvested in October; distilling of the wine made from them begins two weeks later—it must be completed by March of the next year. The wine is distilled twice in a *charentais* still handmade from copper, the only sort of still authorized by French regulations. After the second distillation, the clear spirit, known as *eau de vie*, is set aside in barrels made of Limousin or Troncais oak to age—often for decades. In the process, up to a third of the barrel can be lost to evaporation. The people of the Charente region claim that they all live to ripe old ages, and attribute it to the very faint haze of evaporating cognac in the air they breathe.

The contents of a bottle of fine cognac are actually a careful blend of many different cognacs of different ages and regions. The blending process is a delicate operation, requiring all the skill and experience of the cellar master to create exactly the right mix of

This cognac, above, from Delamain is labeled "pale and dry," which means it is the youngest made by the firm. Young is a relative term, however; all the cognacs used in the blend are at least twenty years old.

139

complementary flavors again and again. The blended cognac is then placed in another barrel and left in the cellar for months or even years longer to age further and allow the flavors to "marry."

COGNAC TERMINOLOGY

The vocabulary of cognac can be confusing, in part because although the producers are French, the bulk of their product is sold in the English-speaking world. For purely commercial reasons, then, the words that designate quality on the cognac label are in English. The different quality designations place a cognac into the different age categories set forth by the French government. The designated quality always reflects the youngest cognac used in the blend; age alone, however, is only one factor in the complex blend of flavors making up a fine cognac. The classification "Fine Champagne" on a label means that the cognac originated exclusively from the two premier crus of the cognac region, Grande Champagne and Petite Champagne, and that at least half is from the Grande Champagne. The letters VS on the label mean "Very Special" and mean that the youngest cognac in the blend is only two years old. The letters VSOP mean "Very Special Old Pale" and refer

140

Courvoisier markets a cognac called Vendanges in limited-edition, numbered bottles, left, designed by the artist Erté. There are seven decanters in the series; this is the second.

to the next oldest cognac quality (a minimum of four and a half years); sometimes the letters VO or VSP are used instead. Other quality and age indicators in ascending order are Extra, Royal, Napoleon and XO. The amount of time allotted for aging depends on the individual maker, but it is often indicated on the label.

The terminology used for the very finest cognacs, however, varies with the maker. Courvoisier, for example, calls its finest cognac Napoleon, because Napoleon himself favored the cognac and visited the Courvoisier warehouses in 1811. Courvoisier also produces the Collection Erté, a limited-edition seven-design se-

ries of elegant decanters designed by Erté. The numbered bottles hold an unusual cognac called Vendanges; the blend includes vintage cognac from 1892, the year of Erté's birth.

Delamain's youngest cognac (aged for around twenty-five years and never for less than twenty) is called Pale and Dry; the next oldest (at thirty-five years) is called Vesper; and Très Venerable is aged for fifty years, the maximum age to which cognacs improve. Delamain also infrequently releases in limited quantities a very rare, very old unblended cognac called Reserve de la Famille; each precious bottle is numbered and shipped in a wooden case.

Fine wines from California are generally described by the type of grape (cabernet sauvignon, for example) used to make them, right, and are known for that reason as varietals.

Cognacs from Hine are designated Antique when they contain cognacs that are twenty to twenty-five years old; Triomphe is used to indicate a blend of cognacs whose average age is forty to fifty years. The rarest Hine cognac is called Family Reserve; these are unblended, single-cask cognacs matured from the harvest of a single exceptional year. A very few numbered and registered bottles are made available every year.

Grand Marnier begins with fine cognac and is then flavored with exotic oranges to produce one of the world's most popular liqueurs. An unusual limited-edition *grand cuvée* is available bottled in specially commissioned Lalique crystal decanters. Only 1,200 of the decanters were produced, each etched with a registration number on its base and stopper.

A superior cognac is judged not by its price but by the pleasure it offers. It must be admitted, however, that the best cognacs are not only rare but costly. Unless you are fortunate enough to have a generous friend who is a cognac lover, you will have to visit a fine restaurant or bar to find a good array of outstanding cognacs to sample. Well-stocked liquor stores with knowledgeable owners will often carry at least one or two rare cognacs, and may be able to place a special order for others. The complex maze of state liquor regulations prevents an individual from ordering cognac directly from either the importer or from an out-of-state retailer.

CALIFORNIA BOUTIQUE WINES

There are nearly five hundred different vineyards and wineries in California. A handful of them are extremely small and extremely famous, with only forty or even fewer acres of vines; annual production may be only a few hundred cases of exceptional wine. Wines from boutique wineries such as Hanzell, Stony Hill, Diamond Creek and Dunn are rare and in great demand. Only the most well-stocked wine merchants will have the occasional case, and supplies are often sold out at the winery years in advance.

COOKWARE

Tom Raredon makes these hand-formed, perfectly functional copper pans, above. The handles are made of forged brass and seasoned mountain laurel; handmade brass rivets attach them to the pans.

The tools of the serious cook are so many and varied, and often so specialized, that there would seem to be little reason for any to be custom-made. There are, however, some craftspeople working in this area, producing cookware that is practical and beautiful.

Karl Schröen produces exceptionally handsome hand-forged kitchen knives for carving, cleaving, and other general uses. After grinding the steel blades to shape, Schröen uses differential tempering to produce a well-balanced knife that is tough and flexible and holds an edge well. The hand-carved handles are made of exotic woods or various different types of horn.

Hand-forged knives, opposite page, carving sets, and unique tools for the kitchen and elsewhere are made by Karl Schröen from specialty steels. The handles and decorations are made to order as well.

142

CHAPTER 8

PERSONAL SERVICES

How much of this bounty, right, is really good for you? Registered dietitians are professionals trained in nutrition and able to help you make sensible decisions about what you eat.

PERSONAL TRAINERS

Personal trainers, once the exclusive privilege of Hollywood's rich and famous—Christopher Reeve became Superman under the guidance of a personal trainer—are now available to anyone. One-on-one training can be of enormous help in meeting your fitness goals.

Personal training is available at all levels, in ways that can meet anyone's schedule, goals and pocketbook. Sessions can be held at a club or studio, at home, at the office, on running paths or anywhere else convenient for the individual client.

At the first level, a trainer can be hired for just a few sessions to help set up an individual fitness program. This works well for the self-motivated person, who then carries on the program alone, occasionally calling in the trainer for changes to the routine.

At a more involved level, the personal trainer creates a tailored program and arranges for monthly check-ups. At each check-up, the trainer adjusts the program, checks for problems and adds new or different exercises. This schedule appeals to those who want to achieve specific fitness goals and will supplement their personal program with workouts in a club or studio.

For the exclusivity and personal attention of a one-on-one relationship, a personal trainer can meet with a client three times a week or even more. For the person with special workout needs and a busy schedule, this approach is optimal.

A number of objective and subjective criteria apply when selecting a trainer. Objectively, the trainer should have training in exercise physiology, anatomy, injury prevention, and monitoring exercise intensity. This is evidenced by certification through a nationally recognized organization, a degree in a related health area, or extensive experience in fitness training. A trainer should also have CPR certification, liability insurance, and good references from satisfied clients.

Particularly if you opt for frequent one-on-one workouts, you will be seeing a lot of your trainer. You should feel comfortable with the trainer—a harmonious relationship is the key to a successful, ongoing training program. The trainer should help you set safe and realistic goals, without promising unattainable results. The right trainer depends on your needs—it's one thing to train for a triathlon, another to rehabilitate an injured knee, and yet another simply to attain a higher level of overall fitness.

Finding a personal trainer can be easy as asking at your local health club or checking the phone book. However, to be sure of finding an experienced and well-qualified trainer, contact IDEA: The Association for Fitness Professionals. The staff will provide referrals to certified professional trainers in your area.

DIETITIANS

The latest medical evidence suggests that good nutrition directly influences long-term health. The rewards of eating right are obvious, but knowing how to do it, especially in light of rapidly advancing research, is often hard to determine. A personal dietitian can help.

A registered dietitian is an authority on diet, food, and nutrition—a reliable source of advice on how to make the proper food choices to achieve your individual health goals. A registered dietitian separates the facts from the fads, the sensible from the spurious, and knows how to translate the latest scientific research into practical uses that may affect how you feel, how you look, and even how resistant you are to diseases.

Your life is already touched by registered dietitians in more ways than you may realize. They work with food companies, with restaurants, in health care, in health clubs, in research labs, and other places. They are also in private practice, giving advice to individuals and families with both general and specific nutritional needs. Nutritionists can help people with health problems, such as obesity, high blood pressure, high cholesterol levels, diabetes, or chronic illnesses, eat properly; they can also help personalize nutrition programs for ordinary healthy people. Athletes, pregnant women, high-stress executives—anyone can benefit from the advice of a nutritionist.

Sadly, the nutrition field is fertile ground for charlatans, well-

A good way to achieve your fitness goals is to work with a personal trainer.

Melody Rogers of Body Mechanics in Englewood, New Jersey works with two clients, above.

meaning and otherwise. To be sure of getting sound advice, seek a professional, a registered dietitian. The letters "R.D." after a person's name mean that he or she has completed a minimum four years of training in dietetics or a related area at an accredited U.S. college or university. The letters also mean the dietitian has passed a difficult credentialing exam administered by The American Dietetic Association. A list of registered dietitians in any state is available from the ADA.

147

WESTERN & EASTERN EUROPE

The study of family history, genealogy, can be fascinating, particularly when the family is your own. Numerous guides to finding your family roots are readily available in any bookstore or library. However, genealogical searching can be a very involved and time-consuming procedure, particularly if the records needed are in a distant place or in a foreign language, or if other complications (and there can be many) confuse the picture. Professional help from a certified genealogist may be needed.

The Board for Certification of Genealogists, a nonprofit organization, was founded in 1964 to set standards and certify professional genealogists. To be certified, a genealogist must meet rigorous standards and agree to a firm code of ethics that includes strin-

gent honesty and confidentiality requirements. The Board certifies genealogists in six different specialist areas: genealogical record searchers; American lineage specialists; American Indian lineage specialists; genealogists; genealogical lecturers; and genealogical instructors.

When working with a professional genealogist, the Board recommends that the client make clear from the outset how much money is available for the investigation, and stress that no work beyond the set limit is to be done without authorization. The client must also understand from the outset that a genealogist cannot guarantee results; the fee is based on the time spent, not the information found. To help the genealogist proceed most efficiently, the client should be as specific as possible

The Family History Library of the Church of Jesus Christ of Latter-day Saints, above, is open to the public. **Genealogists often start their research with heirlooms such as this family record, opposite page.**

about what branch of the family is to be studied, and should provide the researcher with all the information already known. However, since much family legend turns out to be distorted, the researcher may still have to check the information before going beyond it.

The Board for Certification of Genealogists publishes an annual roster of members, organized by state and specialty. Many libraries, historical societies, and genealogical societies will have the current roster. It is also available to individuals for a modest fee; write to the Board for details.

148

The ancient and honorable art of astrology has been practiced ever since Babylonian times. Astrology remains influential today, affecting the daily decisions of millions. There are many practitioners of astrology, but very few have attained the level of serious training and expertise needed to create a truly reliable individual astrological chart and give worthwhile advice on the basis of it. Because an accurate astrological chart requires an exact knowledge of the subject's date and place of birth, anything short of a detailed personal chart prepared by an experienced professional is basically worthless. To be sure that the astrologer you choose is qualified, he or she should be a full member of the American Federation of Astrologers. This organization, incorporated in Washington, D.C., on 4 May 1938, at 11:38 A.M. EST, has an established code of ethics and standards of practice to which members agree to adhere. The AFA also sponsors a series of rigorous examinations and awards certificates of competence and proficiency.

According to well-known astrologer Katherine de Jersey, the ancients devised a system whereby the orbital circle of the sun (the ecliptic) was divided into twelve equal parts, or zodiacal signs, each dominated by a particular planet. Astrology is the prediction of earthly and human events based upon the movements of the sun, moon, and planets in the heavens. De Jersey points out that a horoscope is a chart outlining the exact positions of the sun, moon, and planets at a specific moment in time, at a specific place. There are more than 1,700 factors or aspects to be considered in the interpretation of a single horoscope. As de Jersey explains, "At any given moment there is formed in the heavens a pattern, or a map, which is ever-changing. Every few seconds, angles form between these planets because the globe is constantly turning. Your twin, born just two minutes before you, will have a different horoscope."

YOU'RE THE STAR

If you'd like to name a real star for a really stellar person—as a gift to commemorate a special achievement, for example—the International Star Registry is the place to go. Although the International Star Registry is not an official astronomical star register, it's still a great way to give a gift of cosmic proportions. The star name selected is permanently recorded in the registry's vaults, and the recipient receives an attractive personalized certificate listing the star and its new name, along with two sky charts that show the star's precise location. Needless to say, the International Star Registry is popular among celebrities; stars are also often given as awards by corporations and philanthropies.

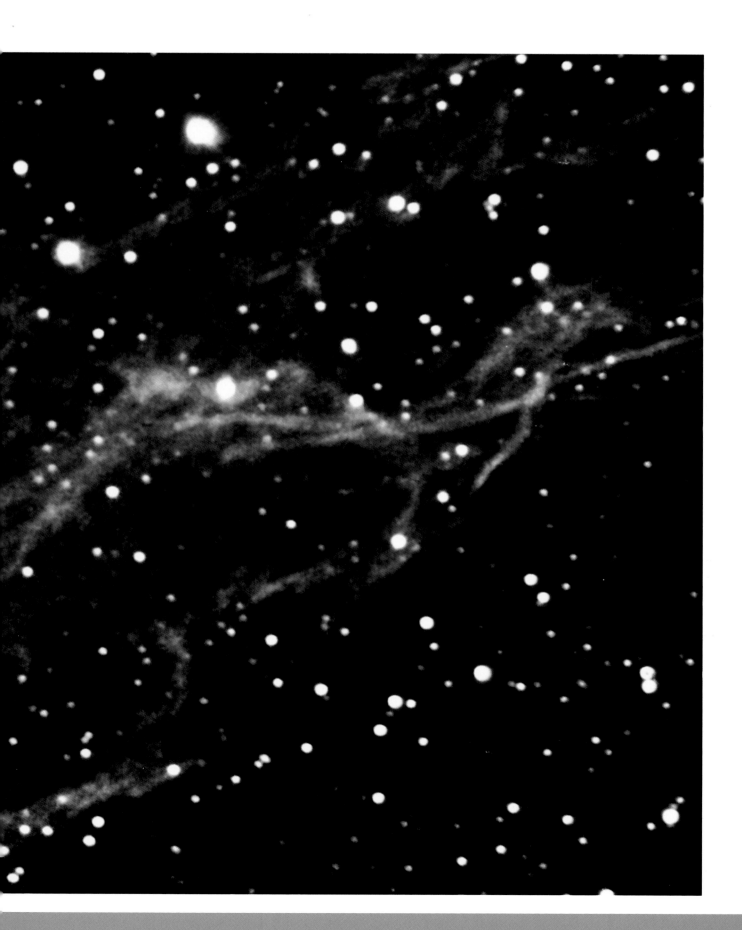

151

The lure of distant places and the luxury of the finest travel arrangements can be merged into one spectacular trip through the services of an adventure travel tour operator. These companies offer intriguing tours—often customized to your particular interests—to remote and exotic locations. You could spend your vacation tracking gorillas in Rwanda, cruising the Nile, exploring the Antarctic, or even visiting with head-hunting tribes in New Guinea. These companies can also accommodate those who prefer slightly tamer vacations, such as traveling by barge through the canals of France.

Regular travel agents, who primarily handle routine business and vacation travel arrangements—vacations that seem dull in comparison to those under discussion here—will not have the necessary information at their disposal to offer a range of adventure tour options. However, they may well be excellent sources of information about the agencies that do specialize in them. Several global tour operators are considered by travel experts to be among the very best: Hemphill Harris, Abercrombie & Kent, and Society Expeditions. These companies offer the finest possible journeys to all points of the world, oriented toward the discriminating traveler. In general, all accommodations are the finest available at the particular location. Tour groups are very small, usually no more than twenty-five, and are accompanied by experienced guides capable of dealing expertly with the smallest details. Because the service is impeccable and because virtually all expenses, including tips and meals, are included in the price, the pleasure of seeing distant places is enhanced by the lack of hassles. Although all these companies offer tours in many places around the world, they do have specialties. Hemphill Harris, for example, is known for trips to the Orient; Society Expeditions offers many unusual trips with a natural history emphasis; and Abercrombie & Kent specializes in Africa, the South Pacific, and Asia.

For the ultimate in personalized luxury travel, Abercrombie & Kent, Hemphill Harris, and Private Jet Expeditions offer round-the-world cruises lasting a month or more by private jet. A standard passenger aircraft is chartered and modified to provide only first-class accommodations just for the tour group—a group of no more than ninety. The global itinerary varies, depending on the trip, but the locales and accommodations are always spectacular.

Society Expeditions has specialized in exotic, nature-oriented trips to remote destinations since 1974. The company's five-star ship the *Society Explorer* visits a rookery of king penguins on South Georgia Island, opposite page. Expert guides and scientists accompany every expedition.

CHAPTER 9

TOYS FOR ADULTS

ELECTRONICS

TOYS FOR ADULTS

The MDR-R10 stereo headphones from Sony are encased in rare, 200-year-old zelkova wood, right.

The invention of the semiconductor in 1948 revolutionized consumer electronics. Cumbersome wireless machines with fragile vacuum tubes gave way to the portable transistor radio, which in turn has given way to the compact personal stereo. Television sets were once half the size of a refrigerator; today hand-held television receivers are common.

What made personal stereos possible in part was the development by the Sony Corporation of microdynamic receiver technology, which produced full stereo sound through very lightweight headphones. Sony's continuing research in this area has led to the MDR-R10 state-of-the-art headphones. These headphones offer innovative, computer-aided design using the finest materials; customized ear pads made of matched sheepskin, combined with a carbon-fiber headband, provide a superior level of listening comfort. MDR-R10 headphones can be hand-built at the rate of only one pair a week, and must be special ordered directly

156

through authorized Sony dealers.

If you're satisfied with the sound from the headphones of your standard personal stereo, you may still want to dress them up a little. Goldin Feldman Inc. will encase your headphones in genuine sable or any other fur. The headphones will still work perfectly well, and they're certainly an improvement over earmuffs.

If you really want to fill your life with music, you'll need an archi-

tectural audio system built into and outside your home (and also your airplane and yacht). These custom-designed systems utilize unobtrusive in-wall speakers that can be part of the plans before the house is built or easily added later. A leading architectural audio firm is Sonance, which offers four different high-quality speakers along with all the necessary hardware; the other stereo components are provided by the client. Sonance

In-wall speakers from Sonance are designed to fit unobtrusively into the home and still deliver excellent sound quality, left and above. The grille can be painted or covered with wallpaper or fabric to match the room's decor.

The ultimate in personal stereo equipment is fur-covered headphones from Leslie Goldin, Inc., right. They are available in genuine sable, mink, or any other fur.

speakers can be painted with matching or complementary colors or custom-painted to match wallpaper designs. The standard grill cloth can also be replaced by fabric to match your wall covering.

In-wall speakers from Sonance sound great and also take up no shelf or floor space. They can be easily installed by an electrician or anyone who is handy with tools around the house.

158

Sony's PVM-4300, a 43-inch Trinitron® color monitor, above, incorporates a digital frame memory for the highest possible picture quality.

TELEVISION

The television set is on for about six hours a day in the average American household. Generally what's on the screen is what's watched, and not much attention is paid to the TV itself, which is just as well, since the design of the

average TV usually isn't particularly inspiring. The designers at Soleil have given a lot of thought to television sets, however, and have decided that the best design solution is to enclose the unit in a custom-designed console. At the touch of a remote-control switch, the TV rises out of the console; another touch and it sinks down again to disappear from view. The Model 360 is a high-tech oval design available in polished stainless steel or faux granite finishes. Other models are made in rectangles, as triangular corner units, in contemporary Japanese-influenced designs, and in traditional European and Oriental designs. All can accommodate a VCR and a television monitor of up to 27 inches.

For the true videophile Sony has introduced a 43-inch Trinitron color television, the PVM-4300. Utilizing improved definition television technology (IDTV), this direct-view TV offers a screen of the size usually associated with projection televisions. The unit includes built-in stereo amplifiers

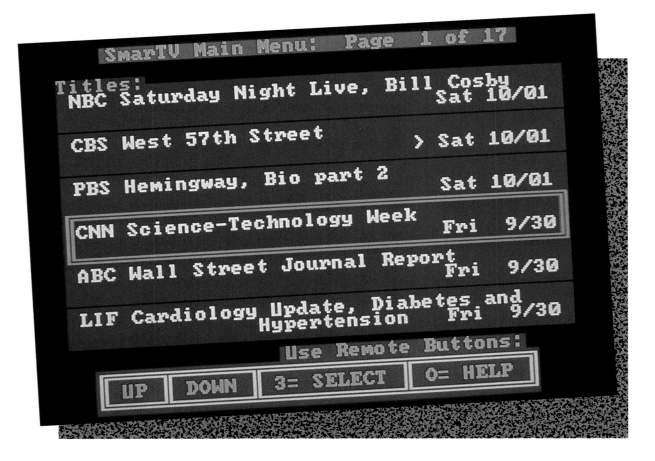

SmarTV Main Menu: Page   1 of 17

Titles:
NBC Saturday Night Live, Bill Cosby   Sat 10/01
CBS West 57th Street   > Sat 10/01
PBS Hemingway, Bio part 2   Sat 10/01
CNN Science-Technology Week   Fri 9/30
ABC Wall Street Journal Report   Fri 9/30
LIF Cardiology Update, Diabetes and
    Hypertension   Fri 9/30

Use Remote Buttons:
UP   DOWN   3= SELECT   0= HELP

and high-performance speakers. Costing well into five figures, the PVM-4300 is available in limited numbers.

Instead of improving the quality of your television picture, you could try improving the quality of your viewing time. SmarTV from Metaview Corporation combines PC, VCR, and artificial intelligence technologies to create "intelligent" television. The SmarTV is controlled by a computer that knows your personal tastes in television programming. It monitors all the local TV channels. Around the clock, and automatically records every show you might want to see. When you feel like watching, a simple on-screen menu lists everything stored in the 186-hour video memory; you simply select what you want to see. SmarTV is able to zap past uninteresting program material at about thirty times the regular speed—about one commercial a second. The secret of SmarTV's operation is a telephone link to a central computer that contains both the coming week's TV schedule and a profile of your personal tastes in television. Once a week the SmarTV automatically dials the 800 number, connects with the computer, and receives a list of all the

The on-screen menu of Metaview's SmarTV, above, is a jukebox-style listing of the shows stored in its 186-hour TV memory.

shows to record. All new customers are interviewed by telephone to establish their profile of TV tastes. The profile can be adjusted at any time simply by calling Metaview's customer service representatives.

159

JIGSAW PUZZLES

This irregular-edge jigsaw puzzle from Elms Puzzles, left, features two cheetahs. Each puzzle from Lucretia's Pieces, below, is crafted to incorporate the client's personal requests for silhouettes.

Generally speaking, the maker of a custom product does not gauge its success by the amount of frustration it causes. However, when it comes to jigsaw puzzles, extreme frustration is the hallmark of diabolical success.

The first jigsaw puzzles were created in the 1760s by a London mapmaker named John Spils-bury, who mounted a map onto a thin piece of wood and cut it into pieces. He called it a "dissected map" and sold it as a simple educational toy for children. So matters puzzling remained until the late 1800s, when the invention of the treadle scroll saw made possible the cutting of intricate jigsaw pieces. A new adult toy was born.

The creation of a challenging, personalized puzzle begins with the selection of the subject—usually a work of art—whose topic has special significance for the client (photographs of family members, homes, pets and so on can also be used). Particularly when the puzzle is meant as a gift, consultation with the puzzle

A Midsummer Night's Dream is an incredible, two-layer jigsaw puzzle, above, from Stave Puzzles. Containing 550 pieces, it is produced in a limited edition of a hundred; each is hand-colored.

maker then follows. Detailed questions are asked about the client's or recipient's activities and interests, and the answers are incorporated into the puzzle as initials, words, messages, dates, silhouettes, and other devices. They're the easy part of doing the puzzle. The deviously difficult part comes from the twisted imagination of the puzzle maker: irregular edges, cuts along color lines, phony corners and straight edges, cutouts, disguised corners, whammy edges (adjacent edge pieces that do not interlock), and other intricately nasty tricks. Even more agonizing are puzzles made entirely of non-interlocking pieces. And the ultimate challenge comes from Stephen Richardson of Stave Puzzles, who has created what he calls the "3rd Generation" puzzle. These mentally demanding puzzles can be put together in more ways than one, a severe test of sanity.

The puzzles themselves are handcrafted to order from fine, five-ply hardwoods, chosen for their smoothness and lack of knots. The interlocking is so precise that a completed puzzle of over three hundred pieces will stay together when lifted by its edges. The puzzles are sanded and beautifully finished on the back. This gives puzzlers the opportunity for the additional frustration of assembling the puzzle from the back.

The final piece of fiendishness is reserved for the puzzle's box—it has no picture!

FOUNTAIN PENS AND FINE STATIONERY

The top-of-the-line Le Man 100 fountain and ballpoint pens from Waterman, below, were especially commissioned to commemorate the firm's centennial.

In an age of word processors, the sheer tactile joy of feeling a well-balanced fountain pen glide effortlessly across fine paper is a rare delight.

After an important deal was ruined because his pen leaked on the contract, New York businessman Lewis Edson Waterman invented the capillary fountain pen in 1883. It immediately became the industry standard, a distinction Waterman pens have enjoyed ever since. So perfect was Waterman's design that the basic fountain pen has remained unchanged for more than a century.

When selecting a fine fountain pen, the old adage "know thyself" applies. Those with small hands or short fingers will feel most comfortable holding a slim-bodied pen, while those with larger hands or longer fingers will probably prefer a thicker model. When trying out a pen, place the cap securely on the barrel and align the clip with the nib to maintain the proper length and balance. The pen should rest easily in the hand with the bottom of the cap resting in the crook of the thumb; it should feel balanced and comfortable.

The nib of the pen regulates the ink flow and its size is an important consideration. Those with a tendency to bear down or write quickly are best off with a medium or broad nib. An extra-fine or fine nib works well for smaller, tighter handwriting. When selecting a fountain pen as a gift for someone else, try to visualize the recipient's signature to determine which nib size is appropriate. Gold nibs are more flexible and conform better to individual writing styles than steel nibs.

Enjoyable as it is to write with a fountain pen, there are some tasks for which it is not well suited. Credit card receipts, bank deposit slips, and similar multicopy forms require the hard impression of a ballpoint pen. Avoid writing on porous paper with a fountain pen—doing a newspaper crossword puzzle, for example—because the ink will blur and bits of fiber will clog the nib.

The more beautiful and rare your fountain pen, the more people will wish to borrow it. Never allow this, even at the risk of giving offense. Everyone's handwriting is different, and each pen's nib wears in an individual way. When the pen is returned (if it is returned at all) it may never write the same way again for you.

The next big decision is the type of filling system: converter or cartridge. For purists who prefer

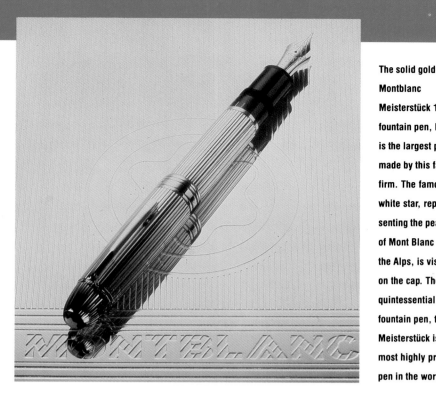

out, always replace the cap on the pen when not writing. Clean the pen regularly, using only cold water (hot water could damage the nib and warp any plastic or rubber parts). The finish on a fine fountain pen, particularly if it is made of lacquer or metal, should be treated like fine jewelry. Polish it regularly with a soft cloth, and carry it in a pocket or pouch to protect the finish.

the traditional bottle of ink there are converter systems, which come in two types. The most common is the piston converter with a screw-driven plunger; squeeze types are also available. (In either case, use a high-quality ink that is low in acid content to avoid damaging the delicate internal parts of the pen.) Those who do a lot of writing or traveling may find cartridge systems more convenient, as the pen can be quickly filled anywhere and ink spillage is not a risk.

To keep a fountain pen operating at its best, use only one hand to open it. Grasp the body of the pen in the palm while pushing the cap off with the index finger and thumb. This technique minimizes the risk of bending the nib. Avoid bearing down too hard when writing, as excess pressure will damage the nib. (Consider switching to a broader nib if this sort of damage occurs.) To protect the nib and to keep the ink from drying

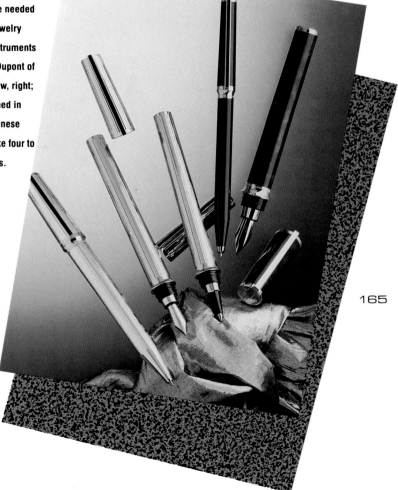

Each barrel in the limited-production Toledo 700 series of writing instruments from Pelikan, left, is individually ornamented by a master craftsman, then signed and numbered.

THE MAKERS

Waterman fountain pens have been industry leaders ever since the company was founded. British Prime Minister David Lloyd George used a solid gold Waterman pen to sign the Versailles treaty. Today Waterman pens come in a variety of lacquer and metal finishes. The beautiful Waterman Supermaster is particularly suitable for signing important documents.

The fountain pen of choice for statesmen such as Henry Kissinger and Helmut Kohl (and for James Bond) is the Montblanc Meisterstück. Crowned with the famous white star representing Mont Blanc, the pinnacle of the Alps, these pens were introduced in 1924; their timeless design has changed little since then.

Pelikan has been making fine fountain pens with an unmistakable beak clip since 1929. Each pen in the Toledo 700 series is individually ornamented, signed, and numbered by a master craftsman. The pens in the Souverän 760 and 750 series are also numbered; producing each pen takes over a month and more than a hundred different steps.

Only genuine Chinese lacquer is used to make the brilliant coatings for S. T. Dupont fountain pens. More than three hundred different steps taking two to three months go into these beautiful writing instruments; the lacquering alone takes an additional four to five months to accomplish. Every S. T. Dupont pen carries a three-year guarantee and an individual serial number.

FINE STATIONERY AND INVITATIONS

After selecting a fine fountain pen, the next logical step is obtaining personally engraved stationery, available in a wide range of sizes, colors, weights, and textures. The cornerstone of a proper portfolio of executive stationery is the $8\frac{1}{2} \times 11$-inch business letterhead, which includes the business or professional name, address and phone numbers, and the individual's name and title. Most executives also use the executive letterhead, with only the name of the individual engraved at the top, for more personal yet business-related correspondence such as letters of recommendation and charitable work. The executive letterhead is always in the smaller monarch size

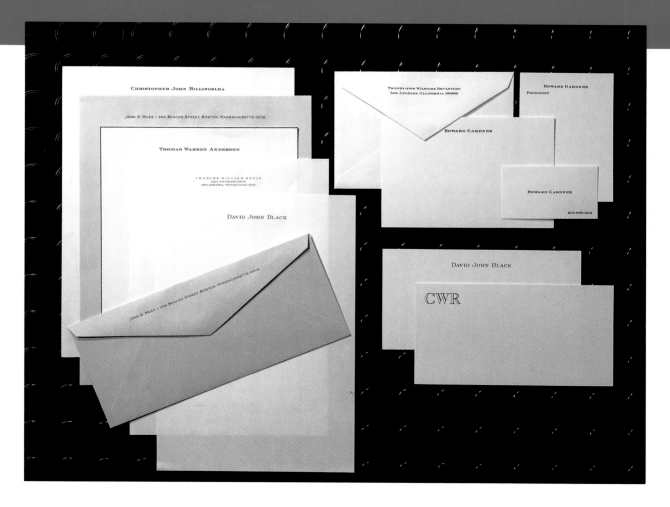

(6 × 9 inches). In addition, a full collection of personal stationery includes side-folded plain sheets for handwritten letters to business friends, acknowledgments of invitations, expressions of condolence, and the like. Correspondence cards are used for invitations or brief notes of any sort, and top-folded notes are used for such general short correspondence as notes of appreciation. Lastly, every home should have a "house paper"—a larger flat sheet engraved with the household address only. This stationery can be used by all members of the family as well as guests.

The finest stationery for business and social correspondence has been produced by Crane & Co. of Dalton, Massachusetts, since 1801. Sold only in leading stationery, jewelry, and department stores, Crane papers exemplify what stationery and invitations should be. The watermarked paper is made entirely from cotton rag fibers, giving it crispness and durability, and the personalized engraving on the paper is sharp and clear.

Two other renowned firms—Cartier and Tiffany—also offer fine stationery and invitations. The company watermark, custom engraving, and quality of the paper distinguish these fine sets of stationery.

Customized invitations and announcements with individual wording and a choice of papers and styles are widely available through department stores, stationers, card stores, and print shops. When the event is extra-

A portfolio of fine writing papers from Crane, above, shows the range of sizes, suitable for all occasions. No household should be without personally engraved stationery. Stationery also makes a thoughtful and useful gift.

special (the Emmy Awards, for instance), special invitations can be created by Diane Designs. This dynamic firm will not only create unusual and memorable invitations, it will even arrange to deliver them by hand—on a silver tray offered by a butler in formal wear.

This pipe, left, made from a solid block of meerschaum, will be fitted with a custom case, signed, and delivered to the client by SMS Meerschaums.

When Christopher Columbus arrived in the New World in 1492, he saw natives of the Caribbean using tobacco. The Indian's tobacco cultivation practices were quite sophisticated, and included most of the steps still used today. By the sixteenth century, tobacco had crossed the Atlantic to Europe, where it was touted as a remedy for all that ailed the human body. Aided by the example set by the dashing Sir Walter Raleigh, pipes became popular, and demand for tobacco rose. So powerful was the demand that it was directly responsible for the success of the first permanent European settlement in America, the colony founded at Jamestown, Virginia, in 1607. In 1612, a young Englishman named John Rolfe acquired some superior tobacco seeds from the Spanish colonies of Trinidad and Caracas. The seeds flourished in the rich Virginia soil. In 1613, Rolfe sent his tobacco crop—only a few hundred pounds—to London, where it was

immediately recognized as outstanding. Rolfe, whose marriage to Pocahontas in 1614 was to bring him more fame than his agronomy, had found the salvation of the struggling Jamestown colony. In 1615 some 2,300 pounds of tobacco leaf were exported; by 1620, that amount had grown to 40,000 pounds.

PIPES

Long before Columbus sailed, Europeans had used clay pipes to smoke medicinal herbs. When tobacco arrived on their shores, pipe smoking became a pleasure instead of a prescription. The pipe itself became an object of beauty made by skilled craftsmen, a tradition that continues today in the finest pipes.

Meerschaum pipes are considered by many to be the best for both smoking and beauty. Because meerschaum can be carved into intricate shapes, and because it provides a smoke that is cool and mild, it is perfect for

pipes that are also functional works of art. The purest meerschaum (technically called hydrous magnesium silicate) is found only in a 4-square-mile area near Eskisehir in Turkey. The lightest and whitest blocks are selected by the master craftsmen, who carve the pipe out of a single block. (It is only these pipes that can be marked "block meerschaum"; pipes marked "genuine meerschaum" are molded from meerschaum powder.) The finished pipe is dipped into a mixture of hot oils and waxes. As the pipe is smoked, the coating gradually changes color—from white to pink to yellow to amber and finally to a deep burgundy—a process that takes many years.

Fine hand-carved meerschaum pipes are made for SMS Meerschaums by Turkish craftsmen. Many of these pipes are produced in limited or special editions; all can be further customized with the individual owner's name.

One of the very finest meerschaum craftsmen today is Ismet Bekler. Born in Eskisehir in 1934, Bekler has been carving meerschaums since the age of eleven. Since 1977 he has worked exclusively for C.A.O. Meerschaum, producing outstanding limited-edition and custom-made pipes. Functional works of art, these beautiful and delicate pipes are more often collected than smoked.

At first, clay, porcelain, and meerschaum were the primary pipe materials. In the 1820s pipes made from the roots of the briar, a tough shrub of the Mediterranean region, became popular because they were cheaper and less fragile than meerschaum. Today nearly 90 percent of all pipes are made from briar. Outstanding briar pipes, such as handmade pipes from the W. O. Larsen Company of Denmark, are available at fine tobacconists. The very finest briar pipes, however, are made to order by Elliott Nachwalter at his studio in Vermont, and are available only directly from him or his retail outlet in New York City, Pipeworks and Wilke.

CIGARS

Making a seriously good cigar is such an involved and lengthy process that it really can't be done on a custom basis. However, Leyanda Cigars offers cigars that are unusually rare and unusually expensive. Offered in three sizes, these cigars are made using the techniques of the best of the old Havana cigar makers. Seven leaves are used in the wrapper, and the cigars are aged for a full eleven years—seven years longer than any other available cigar.

Handsome lighters from S.T. Dupont of Paris, above, are beautifully crafted works of functional jewelry. The slim and elegant lighters shown here are gold- or silver-plated. Dupont also makes fine lighters using genuine Chinese lacquer.

LIGHTERS

Some purists hold that a fine pipe or cigar should be lit with a plain wooden kitchen match. Most others, however, think that an equally fine lighter is more appropriate. Lighters from Alfred Dunhill offer classic styling that can be customized with engraving. S. T. Dupont makes exquisitely beautiful lacquered lighters, each handcrafted and individually numbered.

SHIP MODELS

This model by Stephen Henninger, below, was commissioned through the American Marine Model Gallery. Henninger's work is displayed in the Smithsonian and the New York Yacht Club.

170

Only one gallery in the world is devoted solely to model ships: The American Marine Model Gallery in Salem, Massachusetts. In addition to handling antique ship models, the gallery specializes in custom-built models. These museum-quality pieces are made by some of the most renowned craftsmen in the field. On each model the rigging, construction materials, size, hull shape, sails, and deck planking meet the highest standards of realism. Only the cordage, chain, and belaying pins are made from commercially prefabricated parts—everything else is painstakingly made from scratch by the artisan. All models from the American Marine Model Gallery are accompanied by statements of authenticity, museum classification, a biography of the artist, and other appropriate provenance information. In addition, the gallery keeps records of each model in its archives.

Owner and director Michael Wall is internationally recognized as one of the foremost experts on model ships. As the founder and former director of the model ship department at the Mystic Seaport Museum store, Wall's expertise is often tapped by leading nautical museums and fine arts appraisers. The American Marine Model Gallery offers an appraisal service for antique and contemporary ship models. Conservation and restoration services are available. Also available are custom ship model cases and free-standing and custom furniture display pieces.

Artist dolls from Avigail Brahms, left, have an ethereal quality. Vlasta dolls, designed by artist Pat Thompson, right, are dressed in rare antique fabrics and laces. Doll artist Marla Florio creates these delightful miniatures, below.

One-of-a-kind and limited-edition artist dolls are now among the most popular of collectibles—among adults, since these dolls are definitely not toys. These exquisite creations have amazingly lifelike features (often crafted in porcelain) and come dressed in beautifully made costumes. They are true works of art, requiring the skills of a sculptor, portraitist, and fashion designer all in one.

One of the best-known doll artists of the many active today is Pat Thompson, creator of Vlasta dolls. Attired in richly elaborate costumes (often made from antique fabrics), each Vlasta doll has a remarkably distinct personality. Ms. Thompson specializes in child, fashion, and bride dolls; on occasion she produces diorama settings containing several dolls.

Artist dolls are produced in very small numbers, and they can be hard to get. Editions are often limited to well under a hundred pieces. Orders must usually be placed well in advance, either through specialty doll shops or directly with the artist. (Specialty doll magazines and regional doll shows are a good way to learn about upcoming editions.) The price of a new one-of-a-kind original can be thousands of dollars; dolls often change hands among collectors for considerably more than their purchase price.

Metalworker Tom Raredon makes traditional Victorian parlor kaleidoscopes. An interior view is shown, right.

For children, play is serious business, preparation for the adult life that lies ahead. For adults, play is an escape from the pressures of life, a chance to recharge the creative batteries by indulging in some carefree moments of pure enjoyment. However, most adults are past the stage where an empty refrigerator carton can provide hours of delight. They want something a little more sophisticated—and many craftspeople are happy to oblige.

KALEIDOSCOPES

In Victorian times no parlor was complete without a kaleidoscope. The kaleidoscope dates back to 1816, when it was invented by David Brewster, a Scottish clergyman. Brewster had a tendency to faint when he mounted the pulpit, however, and eventually he redirected his career into natural philosophy. His invention was intended to help study the physics of reflection, refraction, polarization, and the optical qualities of crystals, but instead it soon became a popular parlor toy. Be-

cause of a flawed patent, Brewster himself never really made any money from his invention, although he was later knighted for his achievements in physics.

Kaleidoscopes are enjoying a resurgence today as finely crafted art objects. Old and new kaleidoscopes are widely collected, and a number of artisans working in brass and other metals are actively creating new designs.

TOPS

The top is one of the oldest toys known; references to it in English literature go back to the eleventh century, although it was certainly well known for centuries before then. Tops today have been given a new spin by woodcrafter Christopher Weiland. His tops symbolize high energy and playfulness (they really work), but they are also works of sculptural form.

His contemporary designs for this ancient toy are hand-turned on a lathe. Their clean lines, fine detailing and component arrangement are complemented by the support pedestal, which allows the entire form to be viewed.

POOL TABLES

The game of pool has of late shed its disreputable image and let its true colors as a challenging, sophisticated game of skill and strategy shine through. The exacting requirements of a fine pool table have always been an inspiration to imaginative craftsmanship. In earlier times magnificently carved creations of fine hardwoods, often with elaborate inlays and veneers, were favored. Today these models are available again from Blatt Billiards in handmade, limited editions finished to your specifications. Blatt Billiards also offers

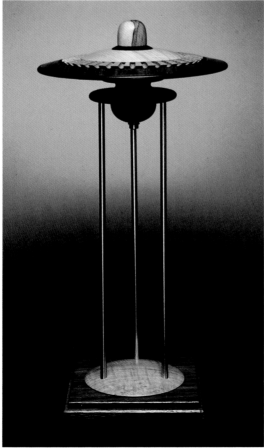

Elegantly recapturing a bygone style, this limited-edition pool table, above, is part of the Brunswick Leadership Series. The exquisite carving and detailing make this a piece of lasting craftsmanship. A toy, but not for children, this hand-turned top by Christopher Weiland, left, is more a sculpture. Weiland uses maple or hickory for the top and pedestal; the tip and stem are brass.

sharply contemporary designs using materials such as brushed stainless steel. Contemporary, custom-designed pool tables are also a specialty at Designs for Leisure. The Brunswick Corporation, maker of fine sporting goods, has created a limited-edition pool table in classic French Provincial styling. Made from select English walnut and accented with inlays, gold, and precious gems, this limited-edition table is custom-made to order.

173

A standard pool table is 4½ feet wide and 9 feet long, with six pockets. The base must be solidly constructed to support the felt-covered slate playing surface and keep it always perfectly level. This means that a good pool table can easily weigh in at nearly a thousand pounds.

APPENDIX

Deborah M. Evetts
149 East 69th Street
New York, NY   10021
(212) 249-7978

Louise Genest-Côté
5578 Woodbury Avenue
Montreal, Quebec
H3T 1S7
(514) 733-8994

Guild of Book Workers, Inc.
521 Fifth Avenue
New York, NY   10017
(212) 757-6454

Minnesota Center for Book
  Arts
24 North Third Street
Minneapolis, MN   55401
(612) 338-3634

Frank Mowery
201 East Capitol Street SE
Washington, DC   20003
(202) 544-4600

Silvia Rennie
Box 470
Questa, NM   87556
(505) 586-1909

Jan Sobota
Saturday's Book Arts Gallery
235 South Broadway
Geneva, OH   44041
(216) 466-9183

Joanne Sonnichsen
894 Ringwood Avenue
Menlo Park, CA   94025
(415) 326-7679

Michael Wilcox
Woodview Post Office,
Ontario, Canada
K0L 3E0
(705) 654-3694

CAKES
Cile Bellefleur-Burbidge
12 Stafford Road
Danvers, MA   01923
(508) 774-3514

Maurice Bonté
1316 Third Avenue
New York, NY   10021
(212) 535-2360

Albert Kumin
International Pastry Arts
  Center
525 Executive Boulevard
Elmsford, NY   10523
(914) 347-3737

Betty Van Norstrand
Four Leonard Street
Poughkeepsie, NY   12601
(914) 471-3385

Sylvia Weinstock Cakes Ltd.
273 Church Street
New York, NY   10013
(212) 925-6698

CHOCOLATES
Chocolate Photos
637 West 27th Street
New York, NY   10001
(212) 714-1880

Gunther F. Heiland
Desserts International, Inc.
Marsh Creek Corporate
  Center
15 East Uwchlan Avenue,
  Suite 420
Exton, PA   19341
(215) 363-5318

**Richard H. Donnelly Fine
  Chocolates**
1509 Mission Street
Santa Cruz, CA   95060
(800) 442-2462/(408)
  458-4255

Teuscher Chocolates of
  Switzerland
620 Fifth Avenue
New York, NY   10020
(212) 246-4416

CIGARS
Leyanda Cigar Company
35 Beaverson Boulevard
Building 8, Suite A
Brick, NJ   08723
(800) 635-7869

COOKWARE
Tom Raredon Metalwork
30 North Maple Street
Northampton, MA   01060
(413) 586-0941

Schröen Knives
4042 Bones Road
Sebastopol, CA   95472
(707) 823-4057

COSMETICS
Charles of the Ritz
40 West 57th Street
New York, NY   10019
(212) 265-2298

Elleance Ltd.
Ten Esquire Road, Suite 19
New City, NY   10956
(914) 638-2022

Prescriptives, Inc.
767 Fifth Avenue
New York, NY   10022
(212) 572-4400

**Visage Beauté Cosmetics,
  Inc.**
9330 Civic Center Drive
Beverly Hills, CA   90210
(213) 273-9550

COWBOY BOOTS
Tony Lama Company, Inc.
1137 Tony Lama Street
PO Drawer 9518
El Paso, TX   79985
(915) 778-8311

Lucchese
6601 Montana
El Paso, TX   79925
(915) 778-8585

Nocona Boot Company
Box 599
Nocona, TX   76255
(817) 825-3321

Texas Traditions
2222 College Avenue
Austin, TX   78704
(512) 443-4447

Wheeler Boot Company
4115 Willowbend
Houston, TX   77025
(713) 665-0224

CUFF LINKS
Paul Longmire Ltd.
12 Bury Street
St. James's, London SW1
England
(01) 930-8720

DIETITIANS
**The American Dietetic
  Association**
Department of Nutrition
  Resources
216 West Jackson Boulevard
Chicago, IL   60606
(312) 899-0400

DOLLS
Avigail Brahms
46 Paul Revere Road
Lexington, MA 02173
(617) 863-8176

Beth Cameron
1000 Washington Avenue
Oakmont, PA 15139
(412) 828-8298

Marla Florio
℅ Thomas Boland Co.
300 West Superior
Chicago, IL 60610
(312) 266-0494

Vlasta Dolls/Thompson Associates
Box 668
546 Gould Street
Beecher, IL 60401
(312) 946-6661

DOORS
Door/Ways
Al Garvey Designs
281 Scenic Road
Fairfax, CA   94930
(415) 453-5275

William Hubartt, A.I.A.
Box 36596
Tucson, AZ   85740
(602) 297-8010

David G. Mulder
Box 1614
2310 Watkins Road
Battle Creek, MI   49016
(616) 965-2676

ELECTRONICS
Goldin Feldman
345 Seventh Avenue
New York, NY   10001
(212) 594-4415

Metaview Corporation
2269 Chestnut Street, Suite 453
San Francisco, CA   94123
(415) 441-6962

Soleil Inc., Interiors
120 South Robertson Boulevard
Los Angeles, CA   90048
(213) 278-9142

Sonance
32992 Calle Perfecto
San Juan Capistrano, CA   92675
(800) 582-7777/(714) 661-7558

Sony Corporation of America
Nine West 57th Street
New York, NY   10019
(212) 418-9427/(201) 930-6432

EYEGLASSES
Multi Facets
339 American Circle
Corona, CA   91720
(800) 777-1409/(714) 974-4080

UnexSPECted Inc.
1725 West North Avenue, Suite 2D-1
Chicago, IL   60622
(312) 278-2300

FIREARMS
Champlin Firearms Inc.
Box 3191
Enid, OK   73702
(405) 237-7388

Winston G. Churchill
RFD Box 29B
Proctorsville, VT   05153
(802) 226-7772

Colt Firearms
25 Talcott Road
Hartford, CT   06101
(203) 236-6311

Robert Evans Engraving
332 Vine Street
Oregon City, OR   97045
(503) 656-5693

Freedom Arms
Box 1776
Freedom, WY   83120
(307) 883-2468

Griffin & Howe, Inc.
36 West 44th Street, Suite 1011
New York, NY   10036
(212) 921-0980

Holland & Holland Ltd.
33 Bruton Street
London, W1X 8JS
England
(01) 499-4411

Kimber of Oregon, Inc.
20365 South Green Mountain Road
Colton, OR   97017
(503) 824-4999

James Purdey & Sons Ltd.
Audley House
57-58 South Audley Street
London W1Y 6ED
(01) 499-1801

Remington Arms Company
1007 Market Street
Wilmington, DE   19898
(302) 773-5291

Ben Shostle, Engraver
1121 Burlington
Muncie, IN   47302
(317) 282-9073

U.S. Repeating Arms Company
275 Winchester Avenue
New Haven, CT   06511
(203) 789-5000

Weatherby, Inc.
2781 Firestone Boulevard
South Gate, CA   90280
(213) 569-7186

FISHING RODS
Per Brandon
17 Grove Street
Pleasantville, NY   10570

Hoagie Carmichael, Jr.
59 David's Hill Road
Bedford Hills, NY   10507
(914) 234-9016

Walter Carpenter
Box 405
Chester, NY   10918
(914) 469-9638

The Orvis Company, Inc.
Manchester, VT   05254
(802) 362-3622

Powell Rod Company
1152 West Eighth Avenue
Box 3966
Chico, CA   95927
(800) 228-0615/(916) 345-3393

Thomas & Thomas
22 Third Street, Box 32
Turners Falls, MA   01376
(800) 248-2638/(413) 863-9727

FLOORS
Decorative Arts Limited
2011 South Shepherd
Houston, TX   77019
(713) 520-1680

Designed Wood Flooring Center
281 Lafayette Street
New York, NY   10012
(212) 925-6633

6: Ilana Goor, Inc.; **8:** Courtesy Sonance; **9:** Courtesy Wendy Ross; **12:** Wells of Mayfair; **13** top: Walter Norton & Sons Ltd.; bottom: Courtesy Giacomo Trabalza; **14, 15:** Courtesy Giacomo Trabalza; **16:** Tiecrafters Inc., photos by Tony Giammarino; **17:** Paul Longmire Ltd.; **18** top: Allen-Edmonds Shoe Corporation; bottom: R.E. Tricker Ltd.; **19:** R.E. Tricker Ltd.; **20** top: Courtesy Tony Lama Boot Company, El Paso, Texas; bottom: Nocona Boot Company; **21:** E. Vogel Inc.; **22** top: Tim Harding, photo by Petronella Ytsuia; bottom: Susan Swain Kurtz; **23** top: Susan Swain Kurtz; bottom: Robin L. Bergman; **24** top: Sharon Adee; bottom: Kaleidosilk; photo by Eric Borg; **25** left: Courtesy Nancy Lubin; photo by William Thuss; right: Randall Darwall; **26** top: Courtesy Chapeaux Carine; photo © Todd Weinstein; bottom: Hats by Sarah Gavaghan; **27:** Vanessa Alssid; **28** left: Scanblack Saga Mink by G. Michael Hennessy Furs; photo by Bruce Laurance; right: Gold Island Saga Fox by Michael Forrest; **29:** Courtesy Evans Furs; photo by Bob Frame; **30:** Carolina Herrera, Ltd.; **31** left, bottom right: Lo New York, photos by Tony Giammarino; top right: Peter Fox Shoes; **32:** Elleance Ltd.; **33** all: Multi Facets; **34** top and bottom: The Fabric Workshop; **35:** Swaine Adeney Brigg and Sons Limited; **38** left: Deck House Inc.; right: Timberpeg; **39:** Sawmill River Post & Beam; **40, 41:** Jill Pilaroscia, Architectural Colour; **42:** Smallbone Inc.; **43** both: Innovative Products for Interiors, Inc. (IPI); **44, 45:** Wood-Mode Cabinetry; **46** top: Phylrich International; bottom: Courtesy of Kohler Co.; **47** both: Courtesy of Kohler Co.; **48:** Door/Ways, Al Garvey Designs; photo © Peter Christiansen Photography; **49** left: Sutherland Studios; right: William Hubartt, A.I.A.; **50** top: Paley Studios Ltd.; bottom: DeKoven Forge; **51:** Robert Ponsler, Wonderland Products, Inc.; **52:** Machin Designs USA; **53:** Lindal Cedar Homes; **54** top: Watts Pool Company; photo courtesy NSPI; bottom: Aquarius Pools; photo courtesy NSPI; **55:** Photo © Balthazar Korab; **58:** Thos. Moser Cabinetmakers; **59:** Sutherland Studios; **60** top: Jim Alexander Braverman Fine Furniture; bottom: Beeken/Parsons; **61:** Ilana Goor, Inc.; **62** top: Edward Wohl Woodworking and Design; bottom: De Gruy Woodworks, Inc.; **63:** Thank Heavens for Little Ones; **64:** Yost & Company; **65** top: Decorative Arts Limited, photographed by Jimmy M. Prybil, Houston, Texas; bottom: Tromploy Studio; **66:** Virginia Designs; **67** top: Wood Interiors by Rodger Reid; bottom: Larry Boyce and Associates; **68** top left: © 1982 Nina Yankowitz; top right: © 1986 Nina Yankowitz; bottom: Architectural Ceramics; **69:** Starbuck Goldner Tile; **70:** Stuber/Stone Inc.; **71** top left: Courtesy Glasslight, photography by Charles Bartholomew; center left: Lamps by Hilliard; bottom left: © Robert McCandless, 1987; top right: Benzlé Porcelain Company; center right: Clear Art Glass; bottom right: Nature's Image Studio; **72** top: Janna Ugone; bottom: Glasslight; **73:** House Jewelry, photo by G. Post; **76:** Beth Minear; **77** top: Lyn Sterling Montagne, photography by David Schilling, interior by Paula Marchman; bottom: Terry Mertz; **78:** Judy Freeman; **79:** Jean Hoblitzell, photography by Raymond Lee; **80** top and bottom, **81:** Courtesy D. Porthault & Co.; **82** top left: Marliss Jensen, photography © 1989 Iris Color Studio; top right: Sondra Sardis, photography by Ralph Gabriner; bottom: The Pillowry; **83** top: The Pillowry; bottom: Doris Louie; **84** top: Jack Brubaker Blacksmith; bottom: J. Donald Felix, Coppersmith; **85:** David Ponsler, Wonderland Products Inc.; **86:** Courtesy Steinway & Sons, photography © Andrea Brizzi; **87:** top: Courtesy Bösendorfer/Kimball World; bottom: Courtesy Steinway & Sons; **88** top: Michael Wilcox; bottom: Silvia Rennie; **89** top and bottom: Frank Mowery; **90:** Courtesy Zita Davisson; **91** left: Courtesy Wendy Ross; right: Courtesy Joshua Hendon; **94:** Kenneth Smith Golf Clubs; **95:** Art Cordiero/Status Wheels and Accessories; **96:** The Orvis Company Inc.; **97:** Thomas & Thomas; **98:** Powell Rod Company; **99:** Brunswick Corporation; **100:** Serotta Sports, Inc.; **101:** Terry Precision Bicycles, Inc.; **102:** Courtesy Cunningham Applied Technology, photo © 1989 Frank Pedrick; **103:** Nike Inc.; **104:** Weatherby, Inc. **105** top: Winston S. Churchill; bottom: Darwin Hensley, photography © 1988 Mustafa Bilal; **108, 109, 110:** Reprinted by permission of Rolls-Royce Motor Cars Inc.; **111** top: National Motor Museum, Beaulieu, England; bottom: Lotus Cars USA, Inc.; **112** top: Porsche Cars North America Inc., photography by Vic Huber; Morgan Motor Company Ltd.; **113** top: Chrysler Corporation photo; bottom: Courtesy ASC/McLaren; **114:** Creative Car Stereo and Security Systems, photograph © Gregg Shupe; **115:** Imaage Worldwide, Inc.; **117:** Art Cordiero/Status Wheels and Accessories; **118:** Corporate Coachworks; **119:** Allen Coachworks, Inc., photo by John King Keisling; **120:** Airstream, Inc.; **121:** Country Coach, Inc.; **122** left: Courtesy William Cannell Boatbuilding Co., Inc., photo by J. Cannell; right: Nautour's Swan; **123:** John G. Alden, Inc.; **124:** Courtesy William Cannell Boatbuilding Co., Inc., photo by J. Cannell; **125** top and bottom: Xylem Technologies, Inc., photos © 1988 Forest Johnson; **126, 127:** Northern Rail Car Corporation, photos by Lynn Irvine; **130:** Albert Kumin/IPAC; **131:** Courtesy Richard H. Donnelley Fine Chocolates; **132:** Albert Kumin/IPAC; **133** both: Courtesy Cile Bellefleur-Burbidge; **134** left: North Country Corp.; **134–135:** Vermont Travel Division; **136, 137:** Courtesy Champagne News and Information Bureau; **138:** Clicquot, Inc.; **139** top: Clicquot, Inc.; bottom: The Buckingham Wile Company; **140:** Courvoisier Collection Erté; **141:** Wine Institute; **142:** Tom Raredon Metalwork; **143:** © Karl Schröen ; **146:** Photo by Mark Hill; **147:** Photo by Brian Rathjen; **148:** Photo courtesy of the Family History Library of The Church of Jesus Christ of Latter-day Saints; **149:** DAR Museum, Washington, D.C.; **150–151:** NASA; **153:** © Art Wolfe/Society Expeditions Cruises; **156:** Sony Corporation of America; **157** both: Courtesy Sonance; **158** top: Goldin Feldman; bottom: Sony Corporation of America; **159:** Metaview Corporation; **160:** top: Courtesy of Rolex Watch U.S.A., Inc.; bottom: Jaeger-LeCoultre S.A. Inc., **161:** Cartier Inc.; **162** top: Elms Puzzles, Inc., © TADDER/Baltimore; bottom: Lucretia's Pieces; **163:** Stave Puzzles; **164:** The Waterman Pen Company; **165** top: Montblanc/Koh-I-Noor Rapidograph, Inc.; bottom: S.T. Dupont; **166:** Pelikan, Inc.; **167:** Crane & Co., Inc.; **168:** SMS Meerschaums; **169:** S.T. Dupont; **170:** The American Marine Model Gallery, Inc.; **171** top left: Avigail Brahms; top right: Vlasta Dolls/Thompson Associates; bottom: Marla Florio, photo by Joan Holzgartner; **172:** Tom Raredon Metalwork, photo © Tom Raredon 1987; **173:** top: Leadership Series Products/Brunswick Corporation; bottom: Christopher Welland.

Numbers in italics indicate illustrations.

189